Vacation Bible School

A CURRENT APPROACH
TO A PROVEN PROGRAM

by

DORIS A. FREESE, Ph.D.
Christian Education Faculty
Moody Bible Institute

EVANGELICAL TEACHER TRAINING ASSOCIATION
110 Bridge Street, Box 327
Wheaton, Illinois 60187

Courses in the Advanced Certificate Program

WORLD MISSIONS TODAY

EVANGELIZE THRU CHRISTIAN EDUCATION

THE TRIUNE GOD

BIBLICAL BELIEFS

CHURCH EDUCATIONAL MINISTRIES OR VACATION BIBLE SCHOOL

YOUR BIBLE

First Edition
Second Printing 1981

Library of Congress Catalog and Card Number 77-76179
ISBN 0-910566-11-9
© 1977 by Evangelical Teacher Training Association
Printed in U.S.A.

Scripture quotations are from the New American Standard Bible, © The
Lockman Foundation 1960, 1962, 1963, 1968, 1971, 1972, 1973, 1975,
and are used by permission.

Contents

Foreword

For many years Bible-believing churches have sought to share their faith and knowledge of the Word through a concentrated summer program of Bible study, crafts, and recreation. Although the concept of VBS is not new to witness-oriented churches with concern for the communities in which they minister, VBS itself is a perennially new and fresh experience. Each year brings new emphasis, new staff, new pupils, new spiritual growth.

There are few church programs which give such opportunities for innovation, involvement, and concentrated evangelistic emphasis as VBS. Those who attend usually experience spiritual growth. The extended time spent under the ministry of dedicated teachers and leaders provides a framework for serious consideration of the claims of Christ.

If you have never conducted or served in a VBS, this book is imperative reading. If you have, you will discover helpful information which will assist toward enriching teaching. It will enlarge your vision for summer ministry and provide foundations for successful VBS experiences.

This book was prepared as helpful reading for church leaders and all associated with VBS. It is required reading for those pursuing the Advanced Teachers Certificate of Evangelical Teacher Training Association.

Paul E. Loth, Ed.D., *President*
Evangelical Teacher Training Association

1

VBS Opportunities

Vacation time is here! Even with family outings and community-sponsored programs, children frequently ask, "What is there to do?" If the church provides meaningful answers, vacation time can be synonymous with excitement, spiritual impact, and growth.

What an opportunity to reach children and youth with the claims of Christ through **Bible teaching and correlated learning activities.** Indeed, Vacation Bible School can have both an educational and an evangelistic ministry in the community. Its benefits are not limited to the young; the program can be expanded to provide spiritual enrichment for adults as well.

HISTORY OF VBS

The origin of VBS can be traced to the latter part of the last century. In 1894, a pastor's wife in Hopedale, Illinois, concerned that the Sunday school was not offering a thorough knowledge of the Bible, conducted a month-long school with 37 children in four departments. In 1898, Everyday Bible School was held at Epiphany Baptist Church in New York City. Bible stories and Bible memorization were emphasized. In 1901, Dr. Robert Boville, executive secretary of the New York Baptist City Mission Society, held a series of schools. He is credited with formal organization of the VBS movement.

Response to VBS was favorable because worthwhile activities were provided for bored or idle children. The movement continued to expand. Here was an opportunity for Bible learning when many churches were closed during the summer months. College students and teachers needed to staff VBS followed the same vacation schedule as those to be reached and so were available.

VBS has grown from a limited venture into a significant church ministry. In 1923, the first VBS curriculum was released with kindergarten, primary, and junior materials for a five-week school. Today VBS materials are a regular feature of many religious publishing houses.

ADVANTAGES OF VBS

The role of VBS in the total church ministry cannot be replaced by any other existing program. Consider the unique features of VBS. It utilizes leisure time, increases teaching impact, provides thorough education, and has community appeal.

Utilizes leisure time

During the school year, pupils generally are activity-saturated. The vacation period, however, leaves free time for both churched and unchurched young people. VBS provides worthwhile outlets for their time and energy. In fact, some working adults even schedule their vacations so they can be involved in this ministry.

What activities are available in your neighborhood during vacations?

Increases teaching impact

Children who attend Sunday school regularly receive 50-52 hours of Bible-oriented instruction in a year. An additional 12-15 hours of teaching is received during a one-week school and twice that amount in two weeks. For unchurched youth, the learning opportunities and loving concern of teachers experienced during a two-week period could be as meaningful as half a year of Sunday school.

Provides thorough education

Pupils who attend VBS regularly are exposed to Bible truths from 2½-3 hours daily through Bible-related activities. Multifaceted learning experiences which relate Bible truths to daily living are available to pupils through a variety of activities in a relaxed, life-related setting.

Has community appeal

The informal activity-oriented features of VBS appeal to parents as well as children—even those parents who might hesitate to allow attendance at church or Sunday school. Parents themselves often are drawn to VBS, either through a VBS adult program, a parents' day, or a closing event.

How do your VBS activities attract unchurched youth and adults?

OBJECTIVES OF VBS

VBS consists of many activities designed to fulfill the following objectives: reach, teach, win, train, and send for Christ. The claims of Christ that are emphasized most will depend upon the needs and spiritual maturity of the pupils.

Reach for Christ

Communicating the good news of Jesus Christ to others is an imperative of the Great Commission. Sharing God's Word and His love can be the first step in this process.

Teach God's Word

"So faith *comes* from hearing, and hearing by the word of Christ" (Rom. 10:17). The Bible, as the name Vacation *Bible* School suggests, is the center of VBS. All activities should support biblical teaching. Basic truths are shared and explained. Faith in Christ is demonstrated so that all pupils have models of what it means to submit to the claims of Jesus Christ. Accurate presentation of these truths by loving, concerned teachers in the power of the Holy Spirit results in pupil response.

Win to Christ

Bringing individuals to personal faith in Jesus Christ deserves prime consideration in VBS planning and programming. The VBS teacher who concentrates on knowing his pupils will begin to discern spiritual needs. He will be able to help those who are at a point of decision and guide them toward personal commitment to Jesus Christ.

Does your planning provide a variety of situations in which pupils can be introduced to Jesus Christ?

Train in Christian living

Effective Bible teaching results in more than mental acceptance of the Word of God. Pupils must apply Bible knowledge to Christian living. The teacher's life example may stimulate pupils to begin practicing what they have learned. Helping pupils apply Bible truths to the daily experiences at VBS is an important contribution of the teacher. It involves guiding them to make God's Word their standard as they seek to live for Christ. Even young children can learn to practice the teachings they receive. They can understand the needs of others, share in missionary experiences, take responsibility for neatness and order in the church, learn consideration for those who are slower, practice honesty, and apply self-discipline.

Send out for Christ

While VBS ministry begins with reaching pupils for Christ, it also seeks to send them out for Him. Children, youth, and adults alike should share their newfound or renewed faith in Jesus Christ with others. An evidence of Christian growth can be seen in this desire to reach others for Him.

VALUES OF VBS

VBS affects more than the pupils who attend. Its value extends to the home, to church members involved in the VBS ministry, and to the community.

To the home

The nurture and training of children by parents who love and obey God is central to the Christian home. Primary responsibility for the spiritual education of children rests with parents (Deut. 6:6,7; Eph. 6:4). However, church ministries such as VBS supplement the influence of home training through group experiences in worship, fellowship, study, and service.

VBS reflects the church's interest in the entire family. It helps parents see the fuller ministry of the church to their child and to themselves. Take-home items, songs, Bible verses, and sheer enthusiasm of VBS pupils communicate the message of the church to parents. Often, VBS provides opportunities for strengthening family ties with the church as well as developing meaningful contacts with uncommitted or unsaved parents.

How can your VBS reach entire families?

To pupils

VBS offers a multifaceted program to individuals of all cultural groups in a community. Bible study, expressional activities, fellowship opportunities, and recreation are planned to meet the spiritual, social, and recreational needs of pupils.

To the congregation

Total mobilization of a local body of believers in an effort to minister to their own families and to families of the community is possible through VBS. The combined efforts of church members in prayer, promotion, teaching, and visitation create a sense of unity and cooperation within the church family.

VBS can help each pupil feel that the church is *his* church, the missionary program is *his* missionary program, opportunities are *his* opportunities. Once a pupil has accepted Jesus Christ as Lord and Savior, every effort should be made to draw him into the church family.

What percentage of your church congregation is involved in VBS?

To the pastor

VBS provides the pastor with a different view of his church family and of the community. He can take advantage of the daily sessions to observe the abilities and gifts of his people and to fellowship with them on an informal basis. Involvement in VBS by the pastor improves communication with those attending. Contacts with parents of pupils and with community families enlarges his awareness of needs and renews his vision for ministry.

To the Sunday school

VBS provides greater fulfillment of Sunday school objectives and use of the Sunday school building and its facilities. In addition, VBS creates valuable contacts for reaching more pupils and families to become involved in the Christian education program.

A Sunday school superintendent strengthens his administration by a careful evaluation of and a serious interest in VBS. This is a great opportunity for discovering and training new teachers. He also can learn from the successes and failures of the VBS program.

To the VBS staff

VBS teachers, leaders, and associates have the unique experience of working together in a team relationship for a short period of time. Opportunities are built into the VBS program for experimentation with new methods and new materials to expand the teacher's knowledge and ability. The attentive teacher grows in understanding people as he observes pupils in an informal setting, interacts with them on a daily basis, and notes spiritual growth.

Leadership training courses enrich experienced teachers and prepare new teachers for VBS. The training experience and confidence gained may encourage some to serve the Lord in other church-related ministries. Many young people, as well as adults, receive their initial preparation and experiences in Christian service during VBS.

Why are you involved with VBS?

To the community

While demonstrating the church's concern for people, VBS acquaints the community with the church's message and services. Racial prejudices and class distinctions are broken down when the church sincerely opens its doors to the community. Many families attend church for the first time because of VBS. The opportunity for church visitation and a strengthening of ties between church and community are developed effectively then.

SUMMARY

VBS seeks to combine Bible teaching with correlated learning activities to confront pupils with the claims of Jesus Christ. Valuable use of leisure time, increased teaching impact, thorough Christian education, and community appeal are sufficient reasons to launch a VBS program.

Objectives for VBS are: to reach for Christ, teach God's Word, win to Christ, train in Christian living, and send out for Christ. The values of VBS extend to the home, to pupils, to the congregation and pastor, to VBS and Sunday school staff, and to the community.

Indeed, VBS can provide the church with a meaningful vacation outreach ministry!

FOR REVIEW

1. Give a brief historical sketch of VBS.
2. Explain three advantages of VBS.
3. What are the objectives of VBS?
4. How does the value of VBS extend beyond the pupils attending?
5. Describe how Sunday school and VBS influence one another.

FOR DISCUSSION

1. Discuss the values of VBS based on past experiences of class members as pupils or leaders of VBS.
2. In what ways should a community surrounding a VBS benefit from it?
3. What biblical imperatives justify the VBS ministry?

FOR APPLICATION

1. What specific objectives should a VBS held in your church have?
2. Inquire regarding the strengths and weaknesses of the VBS program in two churches and compare findings.

Initial Planning

Careful planning and preparation are key ingredients for a successful VBS. When carried out by dedicated personnel who are guided by the Holy Spirit, the purposes of VBS will be fulfilled.

Planning should begin several months before VBS opens. Clarification of objectives in the early stages of planning influences the direction of all other decisions.

After objectives are determined, specifics such as basic preparation, the type of school, time, daily schedule, places, and finances of the VBS program can be decided and planned.

BASIC PREPARATION

Two major steps in the initial basic preparation are securing approval for VBS and appointing a planning committee.

Secure approval

Regardless of who initiates the idea of conducting VBS, approval and endorsement should be secured from the church board which schedules church events and approves key leadership. This official group may be the deacon board, the advisory board, the elders, the board of Christian education, or the Sunday school executive committee. The pastor may want to present the plan to the group himself, or he may invite a VBS enthusiast to do so. Offering a comprehensive picture of the VBS plan is essential for maximum cooperation and support.

Appoint planning committee

Once approval is obtained, a VBS planning committee is needed to care for details. The number on the committee will vary depending on the size of the church and the anticipated enrollment. The key figure on the planning committee and in the VBS staff is the director. Upon his shoulders rests the success or failure of VBS, its spiritual impact, and its appeal for worker and financial support.

Others on the committee include an assistant director capable of assuming leadership in a future VBS, a secretary, a treasurer, and department superintendents. Each of these needs an understanding of and a dedication to the task of planning and administering an effective VBS.

Who qualifies for VBS planning committee membership in your church?

During the early months of preparation, monthly planning meetings may be sufficient. As the opening date approaches, more frequent meetings must be held. If dates are set early and made known to those involved, many conflicting dates can be avoided.

Responsibilities of the planning committee are both direct and indirect. Areas where the committee is immediately involved are direct responsibilities. The following chart lists these areas and corresponding chapters in this book where more detailed information is given about each.

DIRECT RESPONSIBILITIES

Determine school objectives (chapter 1)
Decide type of school (chapter 2)
Plan school timing (chapter 2)
Set up VBS calendar (chapter 2)
Select curriculum (chapter 3)
Establish grouping system (chapter 4)
Organize record system (chapters 4, 7)
Select VBS workers (chapter 5)
Conduct evaluation (chapter 12)

Planning and preparation details which the committee delegates to other individuals or committees are indirect responsibilities. These responsibilities and the chapters giving more specific information about them are listed below.

INDIRECT RESPONSIBILITIES

Plan facilities (chapter 2)
Obtain equipment and supplies (chapter 4)
Determine transportation (chapter 4)

Train leadership (chapter 5)
Organize dedication service (chapter 5)
Promote VBS (chapter 6)
Decide upon closing program (chapter 12)
Plan follow-up (chapter 12)

TYPE OF SCHOOL

Organization and sponsorship of VBS programs may have varied and unique features, but there are basic similarities. Location, needs, and objectives determine the most suitable type of school.

Individual church school

Most popular is the individual church school where a church is entirely responsible for its leadership, choice of curriculum, staffing, organization, and finances. The church has sole control and can promote its own local church and missionary program as well as follow up VBS prospects for fuller church involvement.

Cooperative school

In a cooperative school, two or more churches cooperate by sharing a centrally located facility and pooling personnel and materials. Cooperative schools are interdenominational, denominational, or independent ventures. The larger supply of workers, better facilities, and combined finances provide some advantages. Better public support from community organizations and firms as well as from a wider range of families may result from this cooperative effort.

Limitations exist, though. Since in a cooperative school all churches share an equal voice in program planning, an evangelical church faces risks as well as benefits when aligning itself with other community churches. A Bible-believing church may face compromising its doctrinal stand because of curriculum choice or selection of workers who do not understand spiritual truth. Where problems cannot be satisfactorily resolved, a church should plan its own school.

Branch school

Similar to a branch Sunday school, a branch VBS is conducted by a church in a different location from its own building. Another section of the city, another community, a suburb, or a rural area where there is no VBS are suitable locations for branch schools. Workers trained, equipped, and financed by the local church assume responsibility for the school. Where possible, however, residents in the branch area are included in the staff.

Variations

Although VBS is usually held in a church building, there are numerous ways to vary the setting. Backyard or neighborhood VBS may hold small classes in several homes. VBS could meet in a community or state park if permission is obtained in advance. The recreation or meeting room of a condominium or an apartment complex is a good VBS center. VBS also may meet in a vacant store, a tent, or designated area of a shopping plaza or mall. With vision, creativity, and determination, meaningful ways to reach a community for Christ can be found.

How could your church extend its outreach using one of these VBS variations?

TIME OF SCHOOL

The planning committee is responsible for determining the dates, length, and hours of VBS. These times should be selected several months in advance and reserved on church and community calendars. Factors to consider include availability of teachers, church activities such as retreats and camp, work schedules of adults and student assistants, vacation schedules, school and community activities, timing of VBS in other churches, local weather conditions.

Dates

During the summer, VBS can be held in the early, middle, or late part of the season. Each time has its unique advantages and disadvantages.

Early summer VBS begins immediately after the close of school. Children are still in the habit of attending school and studying. It is likely that the weather is milder at this time, making teaching and studying easier. On the other hand, children may be tired of the school atmosphere. Also, summer school and community programs such as music and swimming lessons may conflict with early VBS.

Mid-summer offers opportunity to relax after school has closed and avoids conflicting with early summer school and community programs. The teaching staff and enrollment may be limited, though, since July and August are often significant months for family vacations.

A VBS program in late summer will fill the need of guided activities for restless children. However, holding training sessions for workers during the peak vacation time prior to a late VBS may limit staff participation.

Holding a program similar to VBS at a different period of the year, such as a winter school break, is another possibility provided there is sufficient staff available to help.

Length

Many curriculum publishers offer both five- and ten-day programs. School objectives and availability of staff largely determine the length of VBS. The school must be long enough to be effective. Christian attitudes and habits often can be developed better in a ten-day school. Some churches offer a one-day-a-week VBS for six or eight weeks. Other churches hold VBS for eight days—one five-day week and Monday through Wednesday of the second week with a closing program on Wednesday evening.

Hour

The hour to begin VBS is largely influenced by the particular situation of each school. Cooler morning hours may be best for both pupils and teachers. Many children like to have their afternoons free for outdoor activities. Unfortunately, few men are available to teach mornings.

Afternoon sessions are another possibility. The free morning provides time for completion of household and other responsibilities.

Some churches plan an all-day VBS, from 9:00 in the morning until 2:30 in the afternoon. Children bring a sandwich and dessert for lunch, and the church provides a beverage.

An evening VBS involves entire families. The program can be geared to family-unit participation or departmental groupings from nursery through adult. Often men can be enlisted then as teachers and leaders. The evening session, however, can be tiring for very young children, and, unless the entire family comes, parents may hesitate to send their children.

How does the time your VBS is held affect the results?

SCHEDULE OF SCHOOL

Many daily schedules suggested in VBS curriculums are balanced in emphasis, educationally sound, and helpful in planning the overall school schedule. The planning committee coordinates departmental schedules to avoid overlap and conflicts with drinking fountain, washroom, refreshment, and recreation times. Include in the overall schedule time for a closing program rehearsal.

As department superintendents consider the needs and capabilities of pupils with their staff, they can make necessary schedule adjustments. Different age levels require different schedules. Flexibility is required for preschoolers and kindergartners while juniors and junior highs can follow a more structured time schedule with varied activities. Older youth and adults often appreciate less diversity with more Bible study.

Who in your VBS coordinates all the scheduling details?

PLACE OF SCHOOL

When VBS is held in the church building, it is helpful to use locations that correspond with Sunday school departments. This provides equipment scaled to size, graded supplies are on hand, and many pupils are familiar with the location.

Arrange for a records and supply office, craft area, restrooms, a place for refreshment preparation, and a recreation area. A large VBS enrollment may require additional space. Classes may meet in nearby homes, the parsonage, a neighboring church, or school. Pitching a tent in the church parking lot or on the lawn provides extra room. When the weather permits, some departments could meet outdoors.

FINANCES OF SCHOOL

Churches that regularly hold VBS usually have a definite plan for financing the school. The planning committee must work within the VBS budget authorized by the church. Costs of curriculum, promotional materials, supplies, and incidentals are included in the overall budget. The choice of curriculum and extras such as refreshments and craft projects will vary with the budget.

In cases where VBS is not included in the total church budget or the plan for financing of VBS needs revision, alternative plans can be arranged. A few possible sources for support include financing by the Sunday school, a special offering during VBS or at the closing program, gifts from individuals or groups in the church, or a voluntary registration fee.

How does your church provide for its VBS budget?

ADVANCE PLANNING

The planning committee needs to develop an operating schedule which includes every aspect of VBS. Set checkpoints and dates for completing each stage of planning. Publishers of curriculum frequently suggest a planning calendar in their materials which can be adapted to individual needs.

Scheduling training sessions for workers is an important part of planning since the preparation of teachers is a prerequisite for a successful school.

SUMMARY

Broad areas of planning must be completed before personnel training, specific program planning, and preparation of materials can begin. Preliminary considerations include securing approval from the appropriate board of the church and appointing a VBS planning committee. This committee assumes responsibility for the details of the school including the type, time, schedule, place, and finances. It develops an overall plan of operation with coordinated daily schedules for each department.

FOR REVIEW

1. Distinguish between the direct and indirect responsibilities of the VBS planning committee.
2. List the types of VBS, with their advantages and limitations.
3. What factors are important to consider when determining the time of school?
4. In planning the daily schedule, what considerations should be made?
5. Suggest three ways VBS might be financed.

FOR DISCUSSION

1. Select a panel of three class members to discuss the best date, time of day, and length of VBS. The panel should be able to support their views when questioned by class members.
2. How can a diversity of activities be included in the daily schedule so that pupil needs and departmental goals are met?
3. In what ways can the results of a branch VBS be continued.

FOR APPLICATION

1. Make a chart of committees which are helpful in carrying out a small or large VBS.
2. Using a specific VBS curriculum, develop a planning schedule with suggested checkpoints until the school begins.

FOR ADDITIONAL ENRICHMENT

Calhoun, Mary. *Vacation Time, Leisure Time, Any Time You Choose.* Nashville: Abingdon Press, 1974.
Self, Margaret, ed. *How to Plan and Organize Year-Round Bible Ministries.* Ventura, CA: Regal Books, 1976

Choosing Curriculum

Selecting curriculum is crucial for it influences the entire VBS program. A variety of well-written, up-to-date published materials is available. Consider the message and its expected effectiveness for an individual school.

A wide range of meaning has been attached to the term *curriculum*. Traditionally, curriculum referred only to a specific course of study. Teachers felt an imperative to adhere strictly to the printed material. Much to their frustration, they either could not fit in everything suggested by the publishers, or they wished to add some of their own teaching methods and could not.

At the other extreme, a more contemporary usage of the word labels all that happens to a person as curriculum. This generalization does not provide enough structure. A framework is necessary for workers to understand the function of curriculum and to use it properly.

Many current Christian educators feel that curriculum is a total program that, with the Holy Spirit's guidance, integrates lesson content with pupil experiences. Christ, the living Word, is presented both in content and experience.

Content of curriculum should be faithful to and firmly based on biblical truth. These truths in turn must be related to pupils in such a manner that they are understood and integrated into pupil experience.

CURRICULUM COMPONENTS

Bible study, worship, evangelism, character building, Christian service, and fellowship give curriculum and the entire VBS program

20

a sense of balance and completeness. If there is a lack in any of these areas, a teacher may want to emphasize some more than others.

Bible study

"Be diligent to present yourself approved to God as a workman who does not need to be ashamed, handling accurately the word of truth" (2 Tim. 2:15). Curriculum should guide older pupils in learning to use their Bibles and encourage Bible study. Provide opportunities for pupils to discover God's truth for themselves. With younger children, Bible stories graded to the pupil's learning level should be accurately presented. Scripture memorization also can be a meaningful part of the curriculum. Key questions to ask when considering VBS curriculum are: How central is the written Word in the curriculum? How are pupils guided through the written Word to Jesus Christ, the living Word?

What methods have you found helpful in encouraging Bible learning?

Worship

Worship is a means of expressing adoration to God and of responding to biblical truths. Often worship is scheduled after the Bible study session so that it can be a genuine heart response to God and His truth. This is distinct from opening exercises when the group is rallied together.

Curriculum should include worship experiences which encourage glorification of God and changes in the worshiper. When worship is planned as a natural response to God's Word and the pupils are involved in the worship, meaningful results are likely to follow.

How can you increase the amount of pupil participation in worship?

Evangelism

Evangelism is central to the VBS program. Biblical truths must be presented in such a manner that unsaved can hear and understand the way of salvation. Bible stories and lessons should be examined for the extent and degree of teaching on salvation. When considering the place of evangelism in the curriculum ask: How are pupils led to a decision for Christ? Is the gospel simply and clearly presented? Does the invitation allow for a natural, Spirit-prompted response? Are effective teacher helps provided for presenting and following up the salvation message?

Character building

Curriculum should provide more than information about Bible facts and truths. Opportunities for specific behavior changes, both in unbelievers and believers, should be offered. Unbelievers can be challenged to make a personal commitment to Jesus Christ. Believers need challenges to encourage growth to Christian maturity. Activities and experiences which support and surround daily Bible truths are most effective in accomplishing these goals.

Pupils should be encouraged to practice genuine Christian living at VBS as well as in their homes and neighborhoods. Demonstration of the fruit of the Spirit—love, joy, peace, longsuffering, gentleness, goodness, faith, meekness, and temperance—by the teaching staff will influence the pupils' personal Christ-like development.

What lessons are you teaching pupils by your example?

Christian service

Printed materials often suggest service projects with a church, community, or missions emphasis. An activity may be a one-day project or last the entire time of the school. Many churches fulfill individual interests and needs by developing their own projects. Care should be exercised in planning to insure correlation with the curriculum content. Examine a project to determine if it reflects the Bible lesson and is a natural response to the teaching.

Fellowship

A sense of belonging and of fellowship is essential to VBS. The amount of time spent in VBS allows many opportunities for interaction. Consider whether the curriculum encourages the proper measure of group and individual activity. When a friendly, cooperative spirit prevails, the sense of belonging to the larger family of God increases. What potential VBS offers for not only making new friends, but Christian friends!

How do you plan for pupils in your class or department to get to know one another in VBS?

STANDARDS FOR EVALUATING METHODS

Including both content and experiences in curriculum provides opportunity for a variety of teaching methods. Quality curriculum is complete, correlated, creative, child- and life-related, current, captivating, conclusive.

Complete

Printed materials should provide sufficient illustrations, teaching aids, and suggested source materials to stimulate the experienced teacher while helping the new teacher. Unfamiliar methods should be thoroughly explained so teachers feel confident enough to attempt them.

Correlated

Coordination of ideas and activities increases the effectiveness of education. Since VBS tries to accomplish so much within a brief time, correlation is particularly important. The degree to which departmental experiences are unified around a meaningful theme each day should be examined. It is not necessary to have a uniform school-wide daily theme. Each department or grade may have its own. Bible story or study, activities, workbooks, worship, songs, memory work, crafts, and recreation should reinforce each other.

Creative

During the school year, pupils are exposed to a variety of teaching techniques and learning situations. It is even more essential, then, that creativity be used to stimulate learning during vacation times. Look for curriculum which gives helpful hints on increasing teaching flexibility and which encourages pupil involvement and creative expression.

Child- and life-related

VBS materials must relate to the experiences, needs, and interests of pupils. Guiding pupils as they discover answers to life's problems from the Word of God is one of the central objectives of VBS. To present Christ as the answer to life's problems, curriculum must correspond to the pupils' level of comprehension. The publisher's understanding of pupils is reflected in the choice of Bible lesson and supporting activities.

How well does your curriculum meet the mental, emotional, spiritual, social, and physical needs of your pupils?

Current

It is natural for school-age pupils to compare VBS and school materials. Most school texts and workbooks are filled with attractive illustrations and artistically presented content. Church materials should be equally appealing and educationally sound. Colorful workbooks, worthwhile handcrafts, and attractive visual aids should be expectations rather than exceptions. With effort, fresh, new slants can be given to solid biblical material.

Captivating

Learning is more likely to result when pupil interest is attracted. The program should flow smoothly from one activity to the next giving variety and dimension to the classroom experiences of pupils and teacher.

Teaching tips, source material, lesson plans, and daily assistance built into the curriculum should show teachers where they are going and how to get there. Each lesson needs a sense of freshness even though it builds on the learning of the previous day.

Conclusive

Lessons must build upon one another in a coherent, orderly fashion. The central Bible truth taught daily should fit into an overall unit of learning that unfolds a larger theme as time progresses.

Are you able to balance the number of new concepts taught with the reinforcement of truths already learned?

Year-by-year development of the pupil should also be evident in the curriculum materials. A progression in depth of Christian teaching should increase with grade levels.

STEPS IN PROGRAM SELECTION

The VBS planning committee must be sufficiently familiar with curriculum to make a wise choice and to introduce the rest of the staff to it. Several steps are involved in this process.

Select curriculum

The director is responsible for obtaining sample materials. Usually preview kits are available for examination. These include leader's guide, teacher's guide, pupil's manual, and sample publicity items. Local Christian bookstores may feature a VBS display or hold a curriculum preview session where a variety of materials are exhibited and discussed.

The VBS planning committee should carefully examine samples using the basic standards for evaluation. The overall objectives for VBS and guidance from God help determine the appropriate materials.

Order curriculum

Check Sunday school enrollment, past enrollment of VBS, and results of neighborhood surveys for a general idea of the amount of lesson material needed. It is better to have too much than not enough so add a reasonable number of extras when ordering. Often, publishers allow return of unopened, unused materials. Order well in advance to avoid the risk of receiving materials late. The leader's guide suggests a time schedule for ordering.

Check materials

Completeness and proper condition should be checked as soon as materials arrive. Then they can be given to department leaders for distribution. To maintain a smooth-running VBS program, a complete inventory of all items ordered and received, the distribution made, and a memo of storage locations must be kept.

Prepare materials

The VBS director and his department heads should be briefed on the general overall program and their particular materials to insure adequate preparation. They should study everything from the leader's guide through the handcrafts to understand how the overall theme fits together.

Actual preparation of materials should begin immediately after this briefing session so supplies for pupils' projects and handcrafts are ready before school begins. Additional workers may help prepare handcrafts, allowing teachers more time for lesson preparation. A variety of groups or individuals can be involved in such projects— youth organizations, shut-ins, young mothers with home responsibilities, and senior citizens. The more people work together in teaching, preparing materials, giving, and praying, the more interest and enthusiasm they will have.

Know materials

Reading the entire curriculum at one time gives an overview of the program. After this reading, there should be careful, critical study. The writer's purposes and the consistency of his following them throughout the course must be evaluated so that personal aims are carried out effectively.

Use of the Bible should be observed. Study Scripture portions carefully, noting the context and related teachings. Passages should be prayerfully read until the Holy Spirit makes them a reality. Reference books suggested in the text can be borrowed from the library or other teachers for further understanding of the material taught. Obtain all necessary resource materials and teaching aids well in advance so there is ample time to become familiar with them.

A lesson plan for each school day with an outline of the intended teaching procedure should be prepared so that responsibilities can be delegated to the various teachers in the department. Memorization activities, crafts, recreation, and music to be learned should be listed so teachers can prepare, practice, and learn them before VBS begins.

These preparations may be part of a training series. Teachers must still familiarize themselves with departmental materials and ready themselves for personal teaching responsibilities.

How can you personally prepare for the important task of ministering in VBS?

SUMMARY

Curriculum materials determine the content and related experiences included in VBS. Bible study, worship, evangelism, character building, Christian service, and fellowship are essential ingredients in VBS curriculum. To be effective, it should be complete, correlated, creative, child- and life-related, current, captivating, conclusive. These factors will influence the planning committee's selection of materials. Proper curriculum orientation and preparation are necessary for VBS success.

FOR REVIEW

1. Define curriculum.
2. List six basic areas to be included as curriculum components.
3. Describe standards for evaluating methods presented in the curriculum.
4. What are two important factors to consider when ordering curriculum?
5. What steps are necessary in becoming familiar with the curriculum?

FOR DISCUSSION

1. How can the six basic areas of need be met at different age levels?
2. In what ways can teachers be relieved of the responsibility of preparing pupils' handbooks and craft supplies?
3. Discuss ways to get fully acquainted with lesson material.

FOR APPLICATION

1. Secure VBS curriculum materials and evaluate them according to the standards presented in this chapter.
2. Outline a plan for thoroughly acquainting each VBS teacher with the curriculum materials selected.

FOR ADDITIONAL ENRICHMENT

LeBar, Lois E. *Focus on People in Church Education.* Westwood, NJ: Fleming
    H. Revell, 1968.

Primary Preparation

4

Preparing for VBS is an extensive project. The time and effort of many dedicated individuals must be invested for results that glorify God. While every area of the VBS program needs careful consideration, five key areas require special attention: pupil enrollment, equipment and supplies, transportation, prayer support, and opening day procedures.

PUPIL ENROLLMENT

Policies and procedures concerning enrollment must be decided in advance to provide adequate planning and promotion. An understanding of the church's resources and of the needs of anticipated pupils is essential in achieving the most effective ministry.

Age limits

The age range of VBS pupils varies. Most churches enroll those four through eleven. Many include junior high, high school, or the entire family. The available staff, facilities, and financial resources also influence the range of pupils to be included. Age limits must be determined and announced early in VBS promotion to avoid confusion.

A variety of curriculum is available for the various age groupings. Some publishers offer material for nursery through adult while others provide only for younger departments but suggest auxiliary courses for youth and adults.

To accommodate the different ages, a church may hold VBS during the day for children and plan special classes and activities for youth and adults in the evening. A family-oriented VBS may be held entirely in the evening.

Providing a nursery can be an added attraction. It encourages mothers to help with VBS or attend classes themselves. However, care should be taken that this does not lose its purpose and become a baby-sitting service for the neighborhood.

What age limits are appropriate for your school to best fulfill its VBS objectives?

Sources

Enrollment derives from five major sources: Sunday school pupils, former VBS pupils, neighborhood contacts, friends, community canvass. If these contacts are developed and strengthened, encouraging results will follow.

Both Sunday school and VBS records provide lists of potential students. Those who have attended Sunday school or a previous VBS know what to expect and are more likely to accept an invitation to attend.

Neighborhood families may be hesitant if they are unfamiliar with the church. However, this can be overcome by penetrating the immediate area surrounding the church with early publicity and inviting whole families to participate in church programs prior to VBS.

Children can be missionaries to their friends and church families to community families. Often a door-to-door community canvass helps promote VBS. This is especially true if a church concentrates on an area that has not been canvassed before.

Which sources of pupils will you tap for this year's VBS?

Procedures

Proper enrollment of pupils and adequate year-to-year record-keeping are essential in a church's VBS ministry. Records provide a basis for realistic planning of curriculum, supply purchasing, financing, staffing, transportation, and use of facilities.

Arrangement for a record system by the VBS planning committee is crucial. A carefully planned system enables the general secretary and department secretaries to function efficiently in their responsibilities. Publishers usually offer a record-keeping plan with their materials.

A good overall system of records provides names and addresses of pupils and workers; enrollment and daily attendance in each department; offerings received; decisions for Christ; curriculum used;

evaluation of the total program; and a pictorial record through slides, photos, or motion pictures of VBS activities.

Individual pupil cards should contain at least the name, address, phone number, age, school grade completed, parents' name, church affiliation or preference, and names of other children in the family. This information may be obtained for a large percentage of pupils through pre-registration. Besides using these cards to record attendance, teachers should make notations of the pupils' spiritual decisions. Follow-up suggestions also should be indicated.

Pre-registration may take a variety of forms. Sunday school and church families may be contacted by mail with a pre-registration form to be returned to the church. Excitement for VBS can be added by holding a special event such as a picnic, party, parade, or program with a time for pre-registration. Colorful booths set up at church on the two Sundays prior to the VBS opening date provide additional opportunities to register pupils.

With the help of older pupils or adults, registration on the first day of VBS can run smoothly. Registration facilities can be set up in the church parking lot, lobby, or various departments. They should be manned by persons specifically trained to handle the secretarial records of each department. Those who have already registered can be identified with a colored tag corresponding to a department color. The remaining pupils can then be registered. Enrollment on subsequent days can be handled by each department secretary.

What can you do to make the opening day registration run smoothly?

Grouping

In general, VBS materials are graded according to school grades. The organization of the Sunday school provides a framework for determining VBS grouping.

Since VBS is most often held during the summer, the grouping plan should provide for pupils who have completed a particular grade in school. For example, materials for the primary department are written for children who have completed grades 1, 2, 3 in school. The following chart outlines the various departments with their corresponding school grades and ages. The numbers in parentheses indicate the flexibility in grouping.

Depending upon the size of a school and staff, further grouping can be achieved by dividing departments into classes. Maximum utilization of a limited staff occurs when the department meets together for much of the period and then divides into smaller groups for workbooks or craft time.

VBS DEPARTMENTS	SCHOOL GRADES	AGES
Nursery	Pre-school	2, 3
Kindergarten	Kindergarten	4, 5
Primary	1, 2, (3)	6, 7, (8)
Middler	3, 4	8, 9
Junior	(4), 5, 6	(9), 10, 11
Junior high	7, 8, (9)	12, 13, (14)
Senior high	(9), 10, 11, 12	(14), 15-17
Young adult	College	18-24
Adult		25 and older

EQUIPMENT AND SUPPLIES

Basic equipment such as chalkboards, bulletin boards, flannelboards, easels, a piano, tables, and chairs of proper sizes for the various age groups already may be provided in the rooms. Other equipment like wastebaskets, erasers, glue, paste, chalk, pencils, pencil sharpeners, staplers, paper punch, scissors, crayons, construction paper, craft supplies, and tools will be needed. Christian and national flags should be available. Shelf and cabinet space and use of a typewriter and duplicating machine can be determined in cooperation with the Sunday school or church staff. Audiovisual equipment such as projectors, screens, record players, and tape recorders should be on hand so that departments can use them on a reserve and check-out system. Recreation supplies and a first aid kit should be available to the staff.

Acquisition

The VBS planning committee will want to delegate the task of locating equipment and gathering necessary supplies. Giving deadlines to department superintendents for submitting lists of needed supplies allows adequate time for obtaining the materials.

Wise purchasing of supplies includes comparison of prices. Some suppliers offer discounts to churches. Purchasing in bulk is another means of economizing.

Some materials need not be purchased but can be gathered by church members. By having "bring-a-supply Sundays" for specific items such as pencils, paste, and scissors, many supplies can be provided. Post a list or let members know through the bulletin what items are needed and where they can be delivered.

Individuals may also share the cost of larger purchases. Families or individuals may be willing to lend recreation equipment or craft tools, or these may be borrowed from another church. Children may be asked to bring their own crayons, pencils, or scissors from home.

Some equipment may be made at a workday prior to VBS. Rhythm band instruments, supply boxes, shelves, bulletin boards, flannelboards, temporary tables, and other items can be constructed inexpensively by persons willing to share in VBS but not available to teach.

Stewardship

The church can be united in meeting VBS objectives through enthusiastic involvement of time and talent, creative provision of necessary supplies, and wise use of church finances. This climate of stewardship needs to be carried over into the daily routines of VBS as teachers and pupils use the supplies and equipment "as for the Lord."

Is this climate of stewardship present in your VBS?

TRANSPORTATION

Although many teachers and pupils make their own transportation arrangements, the VBS planning committee should appoint someone to determine transportation needs and ways to meet them. Inquiry can be made during pre-registration. Once the needs are discovered, they can be charted on a community map and transportation routes determined. A church van or bus, car pools, or public transportation can cover the routes.

Properly licensed vehicles and competent drivers, each with adequate insurance coverage, are necessary. Runs should start early enough to cover the route without a feeling of tension or need for haste.

In all transportation matters from boarding and exiting vehicles to locking doors and fastening seat belts, every safety measure should be observed. Overcrowding of cars, buses, and vans must be avoided to create proper conditions for the driver. It is helpful to have crossing guards stationed at corners near the church and to designate a special section of the parking lot for the pick up and discharge of pupils.

What safety measures has your church been observing?

PRAYER SUPPORT

The spiritual preparation of teachers, workers, and pupils is vital to a meaningful school. Planning and preparation start with prayer for guidance and for wisdom. Individual staff members prepare through daily prayer confident that the Holy Spirit "will guide you into all truth" (John 16:13). They must draw upon God's strength for each responsibility. He promises, "He gives strength to the weary, and to him who lacks might He increases power" (Isa. 40:29).

The VBS staff, with the support of the church, needs to seek the Lord's preparation of pupils' hearts. Staff members may want to choose prayer partners. A variety of methods can be used to involve the entire church: organize prayer groups, put prayer reminders on the church bulletin board, hold home prayer meetings, use the midweek service or a special meeting for prayer, invite shut-ins to be prayer warriors at home. During VBS, the staff should also meet for prayer before each day's session. The time spent in prayer preparation will be evidenced in the spirit and results of VBS.

OPENING DAY

Preparations should be completed at least a day before VBS opens. Rooms should be set up the day before so everything is in place for the opening day. Each class should be equipped with all the needed materials, manuals, workbooks. Extra supplies should be accessible if the anticipated enrollment is exceeded.

The general superintendent should check last minute details with his key assistants. Transportation plans need to be finalized. Attendance record forms should be ready for distribution early on opening day. Registration procedures should be clearly understood by those who enroll pupils. The kitchen crew should have a refreshment distribution plan.

Pupils quickly sense a teacher's preparedness, or lack of it. They sense the freedom of a teacher who has spent enough time in preparation to freely interact with pupils. Indeed, attitudes formed the first day have a lasting impression; they influence behavior during the rest of VBS.

SUMMARY

Preparation energizes planning ideas. Careful preparation for pupil enrollment, equipment and supplies, transportation, prayer support, and opening session details is essential. Age limits of the school must be decided. As various sources are tapped for potential pupils, proper enrollment procedures with adequate record-keeping should follow. Careful grouping of pupils insures maximum teacher-pupil interaction. Equipment and supplies are necessary for teachers to have adequate teaching tools. An efficient transportation system requires early determination of needs. If all the details are prepared in advance, the opening day will run more smoothly. As the church bathes these preparations in prayer, God's blessing on VBS will be evident.

FOR REVIEW

1. Name at least four major enrollment sources for VBS.
2. Identify the basic VBS departments from nursery through adult with their corresponding school grades and ages.
3. What is the best way to allocate Sunday school classroom space for VBS classes?
4. Suggest at least five ways for obtaining needed equipment and supplies.
5. What precautions should be taken to insure safe transportation of VBS pupils?

FOR DISCUSSION

1. How can enrollment be handled so that it does not disrupt the school?
2. What is the most effective way to group children in VBS?
3. Discuss ways to organize prayer support for VBS.

FOR APPLICATION

1. In any church which has held a VBS, estimate the potential enrollment based on Sunday school and previous VBS registration files, surveys, and other sources of VBS contacts.
2. Work out a complete listing of equipment and supplies needed for one VBS department of twenty pupils.

FOR ADDITIONAL ENRICHMENT

Daniel, Eleanor. *Vacation Bible School Ideas.* Cincinnati: Standard Publishing, 1977.

Personnel Involvement

5

Careful and prayerful search for the most qualified personnel is necessary if the staff is to accomplish the goals and objectives of VBS. Planning and preparation remain lifeless details until energized by people who can work together as a team.

DISCOVER PERSONNEL

Many avenues of service are available in VBS. The planning committee has responsibility to find dedicated people to serve. Individual staff members must know Christ as Savior, be guided by biblical principles, and be led by the Holy Spirit. They should also possess a willingness to work toward the school's objectives.

Personal qualifications

There are many qualifications to be considered in selecting personnel. Since not all potential workers are equally prepared, those with the best qualifications should be used. The church should train those who need help so they also will be able to serve.

Growth in experience with the Lord and of obedience to the Word of God in daily living are primary requirements. A VBS worker cannot be spiritually effective without a personal relationship with God. Indeed, the work of the Holy Spirit in the hearts and lives of pupils can only be accomplished through leaders who have a vital experience of newness of life in Jesus Christ. Then the worker will be enthusiastic about sharing Christ with pupils.

Although educational requirements vary with the position, each worker needs to adapt his knowledge of teaching/learning principles to the age group with whom he is working. In addition, a worker should be familiar with the home and church experiences of his pupils as well as their individual activities and development.

When seeking personnel, it is essential to know the specific needs of the entire VBS program. Plan an overview of each department showing the number of pupils anticipated, number of workers needed to adequately teach these pupils, and various job responsibilities within the department.

A junior department with 40 pupils, for instance, would need a department superintendent, department secretary, and six teachers. The craft and recreation coordinators may be teachers or additional staff.

How are workers to be found? The most productive source is last year's VBS staff. The success of one year's program influences the next. When those serving on the VBS staff have enough training to accomplish goals and experience to function effectively, they are more likely to serve again. Each staff member should be contacted personally to discuss involvement and to determine whether the position held the previous year or another one is preferred.

A variety of other sources can be contacted. Most Sunday school teachers already have educational know-how and have demonstrated interest in teaching. Concerned parents as well as older youth and college students may have an interest in and aptitude for teaching or other VBS ministry. New members in the church often find the team ministry helpful in getting acquainted with other church members. Often those who are unable to teach during the year will respond to the short-term appeal of VBS.

What sources of personnel have you been able to tap?

ENLIST PERSONNEL

Planning ahead helps insure success. The recruitment process must begin early enough to staff each department and to allow time for adequate training.

Luke 6:12, 13 suggests how Jesus recruited. He prayed about the selection of disciples. He chose workers to meet predetermined standards and then challenged them with the importance of their task. Methods for enlisting VBS personnel today might follow this example. God's guidance in the search for workers is imperative. ". . . The harvest is plentiful, but the workers are few. Therefore beseech the Lord of the harvest to send out workers into His harvest" (Matt. 9:37, 38).

If VBS publicity is begun at least three months in advance, prospective staff will be aware of the details. Pulpit and bulletin announcements alert the church family to personnel needs. Use a questionnaire listing various opportunities of ministry in VBS and invite others to serve. Follow up each response with personal contact. Department superintendents and other key VBS personnel can share this responsibility.

When recruiting staff, responsibilities for each position should be explained enthusiastically and completely. The prospect's relationship within the department and other information to orient him should be given. Let him examine the materials he will be using and inform him of the training sessions planned. Prayer with the prospect after this session is valuable. Then allow the individual time to study the materials and pray about his decision.

How were you recruited for teaching?

TRAIN PERSONNEL

Effective training determines the success of a VBS program. Both group and personal training are essential. Group training includes general sessions held with the entire VBS staff and departmental sessions. Personal training refers to the individual preparation undertaken by each worker.

Group training

Several training sessions should be planned during the weeks prior to the opening of VBS. These sessions may be held once a week or concentrated into one or two weekends. The VBS superintendent is the most likely person to lead the sessions. However, an outside individual may be brought in if he is acquainted with both the curriculum selected and the church/community situation.

To familiarize the staff with the environment in which they will teach, hold the meetings at the site selected for VBS. Departmental meetings should move to their assigned VBS classrooms. This provides time and opportunity to discover the potential of the surroundings.

General sessions

Allow time to introduce the entire staff so a sense of unity can be developed. Present the school aims, the course theme, and theme song to help members of the VBS team sense their part in a unified effort.

In general staff sessions, outline all the procedures. Schedule the starting and closing times, refreshments, recreation, and washroom times. In addition, acquaint the staff with the overall missions emphasis. Department leaders can share specific ways to implement the missions project in a later general meeting. The record system should be explained by the general secretary with special emphasis on enrollment, attendance, and decisions. Details about transportation should be outlined. The entire staff should be made aware of church insurance policies, use of parent permission slips, and safety procedures. Since the first and last days of VBS deviate from the usual routine, they should be thoroughly discussed by the entire staff and individual departments to insure smooth opening and closing sessions. A general plan for the closing program should be presented for initial consideration.

Departmental sessions

A discussion of age-level characteristics and the learning process is essential for each department. Questions to consider include: What are the pupils like? What kind of activities do they need? How do they think? What kind of learning response can they give? What motivates them? How can they become involved with the Word of God? Examine the department theme and session aims thoroughly to guide teachers in meeting the needs of the pupils.

Sufficient time should be spent discussing how to lead a pupil to Christ. This is discussed in chapter 12 of this book. Choose a simple plan. Divide into groups of two with one teacher taking the role of a student who desires to receive Christ as Savior, and the other teacher guiding in the decision. Switch roles so each can act as teacher. Groups of three may also be used with one person observing. This person may offer suggestions for a more realistic and effective situation. Attention should be given to lessons which particularly emphasize salvation. Discuss ways the department will provide opportunity to receive Christ and how to follow up those who make decisions.

Departmental music should be learned together. Memorization of the Bible passages can be encouraged as personal preparation. Several teachers might practice-teach some Bible lessons to the entire group. Teaching should be demonstrated initially by a qualified teacher who exhibits good teaching principles. Less experienced teachers can then emulate this example.

Various departmental responsibilities can be divided among the staff. A chart distributed to each worker will help him know how and when he fits into the daily schedule. Assign several workbook lessons to be completed for each training session. Analyze and discuss the lessons for difficulty of language, unclear questions, and variations in answers. All the handwork or craft projects should be completed during the departmental sessions so that difficulties can be anticipated and solved. Closing program ideas should also be considered and selected.

Are you enthused about opportunities available in VBS?

Personal training

In the final analysis, each teacher is responsible for his own personal development. He prepares himself spiritually by maintaining a continual, growing relationship with God through Bible study and prayer. He needs to diligently study daily lessons, learn memory passages, and prepare specifically for responsibilities assigned to him. During VBS, he should be alert to new insights about his pupils.

SUPERVISE PERSONNEL

Improving the effectiveness of personnel requires sensitivity to the people involved. Not only should individuals have a sense of accomplishment and satisfaction, but the VBS staff and church should feel a harmonious team spirit.

Build relationships

The development of good interpersonal relationships helps make VBS a positive experience for all involved. The VBS director can be an encourager and morale-builder. His spiritual attitude often sets the tone for the entire school. The pastor's active interest in VBS and his support of the staff's ministry do much to create a total church team spirit. Even if he does not teach, his presence and encouraging words are appreciated. Visits by members of the official church board and the Sunday school superintendent can strengthen the relationship between VBS and other ministries of the church.

Dedicate ministry

To unite VBS workers, set them apart for Christian service, and enlist the cooperation of the entire congregation, a dedication service may be conducted on a Sunday prior to VBS. The charge from the pastor demonstrates the seriousness of the task to the staff and the congregation.

Recognize service

Public and personal recognition of the VBS staff may be given after VBS is completed. Inform the entire church family of those serving in VBS through a church bulletin or newsletter. A special recognition service might be held where the pastor, an official board member, a parent, and/or several pupils express appreciation.

Following the service, a reception can be held with the workers as guests of honor.

The department superintendents and the VBS director may wish to send personal notes of thanks for a job well done. A small gift, such as a booklet, may be given by the church. Expressions of appreciation and recognition increase the desire to serve again in the future.

In what ways has your church expressed appreciation to its VBS staff?

PERSONNEL RESPONSIBILITIES

VBS personnel consists of administrators, teachers, and supporters. A job description clearly outlining responsibilities should be shared with each.

Administrators

Administrators are responsible for organizing, planning, motivating, and coordinating VBS activities. The director, assistant director, and department superintendents belong in this category.

The *VBS director* assigns duties to various workers and committees while guiding the overall school progress. Before VBS begins, this person works with the VBS planning committee to carry out the complete schedule of plans and preparations.

Duties of the director during VBS include:

Maintain daily time schedules

Supervise keeping of records

Visit departments and counsel with teachers

Cultivate spirit of enthusiasm among leaders and pupils

Promote contests and plan awards

Encourage and attend daily staff prayer meetings

Direct plans for closing program

After VBS the director's responsibilities are:

Properly recognize and thank VBS staff

Arrange distribution of follow-up information to proper individuals and committees

Supervise filing of ideas and information for future use

An active, capable *assistant director* shares responsibilities with the director. In some schools, this is in-service training for future directorship.

The *department superintendent* needs to:

Organize and administer department

Enlist teachers

Attend general staff meetings

Arrange and conduct departmental staff meetings

Supply teaching aids and materials
Plan department schedule to coordinate with overall schedule

Which persons in your church are qualified to be administrators?

Teachers

The teaching staff is the core of VBS. Teachers directly influence the lives of the pupils. They should know how to teach the Bible, tell stories, use visual aids, guide in learning activities, and help in any situation with their assigned age groups. This requires commitment and involvement with the pupils.

Supporters

Other capable staff are needed to supplement the work of administrators and teachers. The abilities and responsibilities involved in each position should be clearly defined.

The *general secretary-treasurer* orders supplies; supervises enrollment and attendance records; maintains names, addresses, and phone numbers of staff and pupils; and keeps financial records.

Department secretaries serve under the direction of the general secretary, record department attendance and enrollment, and contact all absentees by phone or personal note.

The *transportation chairman* plans transportation routes, arranges for vehicles, assigns pupils to drivers, and oversees the transportation plan before and during VBS.

Consolidation of ability, talent, and effort can be achieved by naming *recreation, music,* and *handcraft supervisors.* While working closely with the department superintendents, these individuals coordinate and supervise their particular areas of expertise.

The *refreshment crew* is responsible for the purchase and preparation of snacks and for cleanup. They seek to coordinate the refreshment schedules of each department.

Teachers' aides carry out assigned duties and assist in any way needed in their department.

Considering your abilities, what role in VBS should you perform?

SUMMARY

The quality of leaders and their ability to implement plans and programs determines the effectiveness of VBS. Personal qualifications include their own relationship with Jesus Christ, their commitment to the task, able use of teaching/learning principles, and adequate physical stamina.

Enlisting personnel requires knowing how to discover and motivate workers. Training includes group and personal sessions. Developing good interpersonal relationships among the staff, helping members realize the importance of this ministry, and giving recognition for efforts of the staff are essential in the proper supervision of personnel.

Administrators, teachers, and support persons each have special responsibilities that must be fulfilled to achieve a smooth running VBS program. When these are accomplished, the carefully chosen, trained staff will be able to communicate the good news of the gospel to the church family and the community.

FOR REVIEW

1. Prepare a list of minimum qualifications for a good VBS staff member.
2. List at least six sources of personnel.
3. Describe elements of an effective training series.
4. Suggest ways to establish good interpersonal relationships among workers.
5. Identify the three categories of staff and the various positions in each category.

FOR DISCUSSION

1. How would a study of age characteristics help a teacher?
2. Discuss proper and improper ways to approach individuals about serving in VBS.
3. What methods can be used to motivate a staff's involvement in a training program?

FOR APPLICATION

1. Plan a dedication service for VBS staff which could be used prior to the school's opening.
2. Prepare job descriptions for key VBS positions.

FOR ADDITIONAL ENRICHMENT

Eims, Leroy. *Be the Leader You Were Meant to Be.* Wheaton, IL: Victor Books, 1975.

Gangel, Kenneth O. *Leadership for Church Education.* Chicago: Moody Press, 1970.

Promoting Awareness

6

Church and community people need to be informed of the unique opportunity in VBS to hear and study the Word of God. How can they know of this unless someone is distributing information about VBS? The importance of promotion cannot be overestimated. Promotion projects an image of VBS which influences the success of the entire program. The organizational preparations for VBS bear fruit only if pupils attend.

PLAN FOR PROMOTION

The VBS planning committee should delegate promotion responsibilities early in its planning. In this way a separate committee can devote itself to ways of making VBS known to the church and community.

Establish committee

The size of the promotion committee will vary according to the needs of the school and the number of qualified persons available. Committee members are needed with an understanding of communication principles; ability in writing, art, or dealing with people; and a willingness to work.

Who in your church best qualifies for the promotion committee?

Plan program

While the promotion committee is responsible for planning a promotion schedule, methods to be used, and persons to involve, these proposals must be submitted to the VBS planning committee for approval and allocation of funds before action can be taken.

A good promotion schedule outlines week-by-week plans for promoting VBS with several months allowance for preparation of media and contact with various groups and individuals involved. Methods used will vary with needs and available resources. The committee can extend itself by involving groups and individuals in promotional activities. For example, Sunday school departments can participate in a poster-making contest while older children distribute VBS circulars in the community. Maximum involvement in promotion often captures maximum interest and concern in the school itself.

How does your church involve groups or individuals in promotional activities?

STEPS IN PROMOTION

Effectiveness in promoting VBS does not depend on the number of novel ideas invented, but on the care with which vital steps in promotional planning are followed.

Identify target group

Objectives set by the VBS planning committee, as suggested in chapter 1, determine the potential VBS audience. If VBS is to be primarily educational, the target group will probably be those in the church. If VBS is to be strongly evangelistic, the target group more likely will be in the community. Attention must be focused on the people to be reached through VBS ministry.

Is your target group defined?

Select media

Select appropriate media to reach the target group and to accomplish objectives. All possible media should be considered. Are newspaper, radio, and television available? What would their impact be on the target group? Which methods of direct or personal contact—neighborhood saturation, door-to-door canvass, individual contact, telephone brigade—would be effective with the target group? What other types of indirect contact, such as posters, circulars, mailings, would work? The promotion committee needs to consider all possible ideas for reaching the target group before deciding upon a specific plan of action.

Which types of media would be most appropriate for your community?

Plan effectiveness

The message is as important as the way it is presented. Together they must capture the attention and interest of those to be reached. What will excite children in the community so they will want to attend VBS?

The proper format increases the power of the message. News about VBS in the paper can be a paid advertisement, an article for the church page, or a feature story. Regardless of which is used, the message must be understandable and clearly present what will take place in VBS.

Everything produced must be top quality. Good writing style is essential. Art work, photography, and graphics must be well done. Professional work is not necessary but an attractive, neat, informative product is within the range of most churches' capabilities.

Provide response system

After the target group is identified, media selected, and message determined, provision for response is needed. A pre-registration form, a phone number to call, a ticket, or a coupon to return can be provided. If people are to respond, the most convenient methods possible for them to indicate interest must be used.

What type(s) of response do you feel would be most used by your target audience?

Pray expectantly

Promotional planning should be kept before the Lord in prayer since sincere prayer with a desire to please God accomplishes much. "If you ask Me anything in My name, I will do it" (John 14:14). "All things are possible to him who believes" (Mark 9:23). The praying church needs to be kept informed as it supports VBS. Through prayer, God can prepare the hearts of the staff and those who will attend.

PHASES OF PROMOTION

Promotion includes three phases: advance, in-progress, and follow-up. While the majority of details are completed before VBS begins, some features need attention during VBS and after it ends.

Advance promotion

Recruitment, progress reports, and target emphasis are the major thrusts of advance promotion. Making known the needs of VBS to the congregation and emphasizing recruitment are initial responsibilities. Opportunities for service in VBS can be presented to adults and older youth in the congregation through a variety of methods as suggested in chapter 5.

Progress reports concerning up-to-date needs, staff who have been appointed, training schedules, and pre-registration information continue to build awareness of VBS. These reports help increase the congregation's personal involvement. As a result, the announcement of dates, times, and theme of VBS—an important feature of early promotion—has more significance.

The greatest amount of promotional effort, though, should be concentrated on those who might attend. Publicity focuses on those within the church family and the community who make up the target group. It informs them of program details, transportation provisions, and other helpful information. Set dates by which various emphases, such as recruitment, are to be met and write them on a promotion calendar.

What specific aspects of VBS is your church promoting?

In-progress promotion

The congregation must be informed of progress during VBS. Facts and figures about enrollment and attendance should be shared with those who support VBS with finances, supplies, and prayers. They may be informed of achievements and problems for continued prayer support. Invitations to attend the closing program to see the results of VBS' ministry should be given to all interested individuals.

Continued outreach can be promoted during VBS. Word-of-mouth promotion by pupils often increases attendance during the first few days or at the beginning of the second week. A special mid-VBS event, such as a picnic, helps increase interest. Pictures and a newspaper article keep VBS before the community.

The events and results of VBS should be preserved through photos, film, and/or tape. These can be presented at the closing program and copies kept for next year's promotion committee.

Follow-up promotion

All materials, such as posters, banners, and circulars, that were used for promotion should be removed from the church as soon as the school closes.

The main responsibility of follow-up promotion is presenting a final report of figures and results to the congregation. The church bulletin or a pulpit announcement can be used to accomplish this.

If a mid-year VBS rally or reunion is planned, the promotion committee is responsible for publicity. Promotion would be on a much smaller scale, primarily directed to those who attended VBS.

TYPES OF PROMOTION

VBS promotion can be as varied and interesting as imagination and creativity allow. It is essential that publicity be attractive and appealing to those being reached. All promotion should be absolutely truthful since the VBS program must live up to advertising claims. Church publicity, mailings, mass media, and personal contacts are widely used methods. They can be adapted to individual situations or act as a catalyst for creative alternatives.

Church publicity

Use every visual and audio device possible to enthuse the congregation about VBS. Written announcements or inserts in the church bulletin should include dates, time, theme, special features. Workers and programs of various departments may be listed. Interesting testimonies of those who attended VBS last year, who found Christ in VBS, or who are anticipating this year's ministry can be featured. Verbal announcements from the pulpit, at midweek service, and in Sunday school should be made. A skit, an interview, or a pantomime adds dramatic impact. Posters, banners, displays, indoor and outdoor signs keep VBS before the people visually. When this enthusiasm is generated in the church, it can overflow to every corner of the community.

Mailings

Direct mail is an effective means of notifying people about VBS. Letters or postcards should be sent to last year's enrollees. The mailing list may be expanded to include all families enrolled in Sunday school. Circulars attractively presenting the basic information can be sent bulk mail. The monthly church letter can also be used to acquaint and inform the church family of VBS needs and progress in addition to pre-registration information.

Mass media

Most newspapers provide a church page for regular and special church announcements. Often a newspaper will run a news release or even a feature article. Acceptable news stories answer the usual journalistic questions: Who? What? Where? When? Why? How? Features are longer, more informative, and human interest-centered.

Local papers are often willing to publish the names of community members involved in events and activities. Therefore, names of key staff and pictures of a few individuals who reflect some aspect of VBS, such as the superintendent registering several children or the promotion committee chairman explaining a display to the pastor.

It may be possible to obtain permission from community authorities to mount a public address system on a car or van, and drive through the community announcing VBS while distributing circulars, balloons, and buttons. Some radio and television stations carry local news items without charge. Others sell or give time for spot announcements of civic and religious nature. Some merchants will display posters. A parade is also an excellent way to promote VBS. Choose a theme and invite all who are interested to march. It is most effective if the parade is scheduled close to the opening of VBS. The route should be worked out ahead of time and have police approval.

Personal contact

Even with use of every form of mass media, personal contact must not be neglected. Encourage church members to talk about the benefits of VBS to friends, neighbors, store clerks, everyone they come in contact with. Extra pre-registration forms can be handed out to contacts.

A phone brigade could be organized using people who effectively communicate over the phone. VBS circulars and information can be distributed at neighborhood playgrounds, parks, and shopping plazas as well as during a house-to-house canvass. Local restrictions with regard to distributing literature should be observed.

Making personal contacts is a ministry itself. Those doing it should be prepared to respond with wise and tactful replies to spiritual needs that may be revealed. If it is not possible to help personally, reference to qualified sources should be given.

How can personal contact be combined effectively with other types of promotion?

Creative ideas

A good imagination conceives many ingenious methods to promote VBS. Balloons, buttons, bumper stickers, puppets, and contests are but a few possible interest-catchers.

SUMMARY

An effective promotion program is an essential part of overall VBS planning. The promotion committee, appointed by the planning committee, determines the methods, schedule, and persons involved in publicizing VBS. Steps in promotion include: identify target group, select media, plan effectiveness, provide response system, and pray expectantly. Each of these steps must keep the initial objectives in mind.

Promotion efforts before VBS begins involve recruitment, progress reports, and target emphasis. Progress reports, continued outreach, and preservation of highlights require attention during VBS. A final report and perhaps a mid-year VBS event are handled later by the committee.

Church publicity, mailings, mass media, personal contact, and creative ideas can be used to acquaint the church family and community with the merits of VBS. Possibilities for effective promotion are innumerable. Be creative!

FOR REVIEW

1. Define the responsibilities of the promotion committee.
2. List at least five steps to follow when planning promotion.
3. Outline the areas of emphasis for each of the phases of promotion.
4. List a number of ways to promote VBS.
5. For what types of promotion should government regulations be checked?

FOR DISCUSSION

1. How can specific information about a target group be gathered?
2. In your community, what types of media are most effective for VBS promotion?
3. Discuss an appropriate calendar for the various phases of promotion.

FOR APPLICATION

1. Write a brief news item about some phase of VBS using an approach that would appeal to your community.
2. Plan promotion for a VBS program which would be held in your church facilities.

FOR ADDITIONAL ENRICHMENT

Self, Margaret, ed. *How to Plan and Organize Year-Round Bible Ministries.* Ventura, CA: Regal Books, 1976.

Program Overview 7

Teamwork is the key to VBS programming. The planning committee provides a general framework for VBS but the department superintendents and their staffs decide upon program details. Thus cooperative teamwork is needed to develop a balanced and effective program.

BALANCED PROGRAM

VBS strives to relate to church evangelistic and educational goals. To achieve this, a balance of instruction, worship, fellowship, and outreach is essential.

Bible study, Bible memorization, missions, music, and related learning activities are opportunities for instruction. Both formal and informal worship result naturally from VBS instruction.

VBS offers opportunities for times in the Word, prayer, sharing, and true Christian fellowship. Not only is faith expressed in VBS, it can be passed on to homes in the community as a result of VBS activities.

What elements must be stressed for your church to achieve a balanced VBS?

PROGRAM AND PERSONNEL

Each worker has a distinctive role in the department as he effectively exercises his spiritual gifts and talents for the Lord. By matching program and personnel, the strengths of the staff are used to optimum advantage. Just as each worker needs to understand his place in the functioning of the Body of Christ, he must discover his unique role in the total team's ministry to a group of pupils.

Division of responsibilities

To achieve a team spirit, workers should accurately evaluate their abilities. Often one who is skilled in handwork coordinates craft time while another with training and experience in leading Bible study teaches the lesson. Someone else, adept at relating to and working with a small group, guides a small class in Bible learning activities. A new Christian many prefer working with an experienced teacher to learn from observation as well as to assist. Yet, a teacher with little experience and much enthusiasm may delight in the opportunity to teach a Bible lesson.

Where can your strengths and abilities be used in VBS?

Once gifts, talents, and interests of the staff have been determined, it is helpful to prepare a chart of responsibilities for each department. Indicate on the chart the time of the activity and the person responsible. Each staff member needs a copy of the completed chart, and one should also be posted in the department for ready reference.

JUNIOR DEPARTMENT TEAM RESPONSIBILITIES

Activities	Monday	Tuesday	Wednesday	Thursday	Friday
Pre-session	8:45 G.P.				
Introduction	9:00 R.N.				
Missionary story					
Bible study					
Memory work					
Break					
Pupil manual					
Worship					
Craft					

How can you best match gifts, talents, and interests with job responsibilities in your department?

Personalizing the program

Adapt and adjust the program outlined in the curriculum materials. Time schedules may seem unrealistic, insufficient personnel may dictate change, or space problems may limit activities. When adapting a program, the proposed change should effectively accomplish departmental and VBS goals and further the achievement of objectives. In the addition, subtraction, or interchange of program elements, maintain balance. How will an adaptation alter the emphasis on worship? Will the change strengthen instruction? Is one area overemphasized at the expense of others? Careful consideration must be given to questions like these. When making changes, concentrate on ways to better meet needs in pupils' lives. Consider the mental capacity, need for activity, involvement level, discipline framework, response potential, and spiritual attitude of each pupil.

Are there problems in your VBS that will make program adaptation necessary?

SESSION ACTIVITIES

The VBS program consists of pre-session, in-session, and post-session activities. All activities conducted before VBS begins each day are categorized pre-session. Processionals, opening routines, worship services, departmental teaching/learning activities, recreational activities, and closing routines are in-session activities. Chapters 8 and 9 examine teaching/learning activities more fully while chapter 10 focuses on recreational activities. Daily events which occur after VBS closes are post-session activities.

Pre-session activities

Teachers who arrive early frequently find eager pupils already there. What an opportunity to strengthen VBS effectiveness by purposeful use of this time! During this informal period, workers and pupils can become better acquainted. Loosely structured activities channel energies constructively and supplement regular instruction time.

Depending on weather and preferences of pupils, pre-session activities can be held indoors or outdoors. If staff size permits, learning activities to launch the day's theme can be explored. For example, someone dressed as Paul could chat with pupils about his plans for traveling through Asia Minor to visit groups of believers. Group games provide an enjoyable energy outlet when each departmental level is properly supervised by a recreation coordinator or teachers on a rotating schedule.

Indoor pre-session activities allow increased relation to the day's theme. Older pupils can work on projects, prepare visual aids, create a skit or an interview to coordinate with a Bible passage, study Bible background material, recite memory work, or practice special music. Younger children can be guided to several interest centers with activities that support the Bible truth for the day. With assistance from a teacher at each center, they can meaningfully explore the theme.

While teachers often need pre-session time to complete last minute preparations and it is more convenient for them if students remain outdoors before VBS actually begins, bad weather or other conditions may favor use of the building.

Those teachers not supervising pre-session activities can set up their rooms, distribute materials, or finish other preparations. This time also would be well spent in prayer for the Lord's guidance and strength.

How do you plan to use pre-session?

In-session activitites

To guide pupils inside in an orderly fashion, the outdoor pre-session supervisors can line up pupils by departments. If desired, march pupils in to music. Whatever method is used, quiet the group and prepare them for the day's activities.

Decide in advance whether the opening routines will be conducted by departments or for the entire school. If a joint opening is planned, advise department workers of the seating plan. If pupils move directly to their departments, different routes for each department should be planned to avoid confusion.

What is the most efficient processional plan for your school?

The opening includes a variety of procedural matters. Record attendance to gather information from new pupils and to discover absentees. Absentees should be followed up with a card, if time allows, or by a visit, or phone call. Indicate progress of contests such as the number of Bibles and friends brought, and memory work.

Some schools express loyalty by saluting the national flag, the Christian flag, and the Bible. If these pledges are used, explain their meaning and purpose. Amplification of meaning through other activities which teach respect for country and love of God is helpful.

Do you find flag-saluting ceremonies meaningful in your VBS?

Use of interest centers should not be limited or neglected because of scheduling problems during pre-session. Theme-launching activities may be used during the opening.

Personal views on worship as well as the size of the group participating determine the timing and nature of the worship service. Only when the human spirit seeks and finds fellowship with God can the opening be considered worship. Jesus stated, "God is spirit; and those who worship Him must worship in spirit and truth" (John 4:24). Realizing truths about God, His worth, and the need to meet Him personally motivate true worship and communion with God. Songs, prayer, and Scripture reading may lead to worship, but are not a substitute for it.

Each worship service needs unity of theme. The theme should vary daily with emphasis upon the mental, emotional, social, and spiritual understanding of the pupils. Use Scripture verses, prayer, and talks that meet the needs of the worshipers. A well prepared worship leader greatly increases effectiveness. Besides these basic principles, further instruction and suggestions are in curriculum materials.

If the entire school meets together for worship, give special consideration to the wider age span. Plan for full pupil participation whether the group is large or small, young or old. Some Christian educators prefer joint worship services to build a sense of school unity. Since worship is a personal relationship between God and the individual, they do not feel that age differences hinder the experience. Others prefer a closer correlation of the worship service with the Bible truth for the day and meet in the department. With this format, worship can follow the Bible lesson and provide opportunity for the pupils to respond in word and action to the truths of God's Word. At times, the building facilities determine what type of worship services are held.

What forms of worship would be most effective in your VBS?

A brief general or departmental report of contest and missions projects progress, attendance records, and other pertinent information may be scheduled at the end of the day to develop a sense of unity.

Post-session activities

While children wait for transportation, several outdoor supervisors are needed. Encourage children who walk or ride bicycles to return home as quickly as possible. Evening VBS requires additional supervision at closing time.

Many workers immediately return home with their children, but staying an extra few minutes after the close of VBS to prepare for the following day or to sort supplies and handwork and prepare them for future use is helpful. In addition, a brief review of the day's activities and impact on pupils' lives keeps workers alert to progress and problems.

What could your teachers accomplish during post-session time?

SUMMARY

To meet pupils' needs, each department must plan a balanced program of instruction, worship, fellowship, and outreach. A team spirit develops when staff members cooperate fully to use their gifts, talents, and interests in the ministry of VBS. After responsibilities are assigned, a chart of daily tasks should be distributed to each worker. Flexible programming helps meet pupil needs, accomplish goals, and maintain a balanced program. Not only will a tailor-made program develop, but the department's purposes will be enhanced as well.

Pre-session, in-session, and post-session activities all play an important part in the VBS program. Pre-session activities offer learning and social opportunities for the pupils and time for preparation and prayer by teachers. In-session activities stimulate interest while fulfilling organizational purposes. Supervision of departing pupils, staff sessions, and preparations for the following day are post-session details.

Indeed, wise and prayerful consideration of personnel and program results in effective teaching when these elements are carefully matched.

FOR REVIEW

1. Name the key elements of a balanced program.
2. What criteria should determine changes in program?
3. How can pre-session activities be related to the total teaching program?
4. State how each basic in-session activity can be used effectively.
5. What procedures help post-session activities move smoothly?

FOR DISCUSSION

1. With the responsibilities involved in teaching VBS, how can the teacher give to pupils the personal attention needed?
2. Choose a VBS curriculum theme and discuss pre-session activities for a particular age group which will arouse interest in the theme.
3. What is the role of worship when the target group is unchurched youth?

FOR APPLICATION

1. Using Sunday school staff personnel, make a chart showing the division of responsibilities for VBS. Add additional names if necessary.
2. Plan a worship service to create an atmosphere of devotion and to encourage personal response to God. You may use curriculum suggestions.

FOR ADDITIONAL ENRICHMENT

Zuck, Roy B., and Clark, Robert E. *Childhood Education in the Church.* Chicago: Moody Press, 1975.

Learning Activities

The Bible is central to Vacation Bible School for it is God's inspired Word that produces eternal, life-changing results. Who can deny the importance of the Bible since "All Scripture is inspired by God and profitable for teaching, for reproof, for correction, for training in righteousness; that the man of God may be adequate, equipped for every good work" (2 Tim. 3:16, 17).

BIBLE TEACHING

VBS focuses on teaching the Bible and involving pupils in meaningful Bible learning activities. This basic emphasis on studying the Word is reinforced through supplementary materials such as teachers' manuals, pupils' manuals, and workbooks. Since Bible study and Bible memorization form the foundation for all other VBS activities, having pupils discover and apply truths from God's Word is an important VBS priority.

Teaching/learning process

Verbalizing Bible truths is not sufficient in itself. The teacher must motivate his pupils to discover and explore God's Word for themselves and be guided by it. The teacher seeks to guide his pupils through three important principles in the teaching/learning process. He begins where his pupils are and focuses on their needs. Exploration of a Bible portion to discover God's answers follows. Finally, he leads pupils to respond to God by letting each determine how he can obey God in thought, word, and action.

To prepare properly for class, a teacher must first familiarize himself with the Bible portions included in the VBS curriculum. As he allows the Holy Spirit to teach him the truths contained in the lesson's Bible passage and seeks the Spirit's power to obey the Word, he becomes God's instrument for teaching others. Personally discovering Bible truths can change a teacher's own life and help him relate those same truths to the lives of his pupils.

Personal preparation in the Word can be followed with a thorough study of the Bible portion, biblical background, and cross-references. Bible dictionaries, concordances, Bible atlases, and other references provide interesting and needed information. Often publishers include helpful background information and suggest resources for further study. With these preparations, effective choice of a teaching method or methods for presenting the Scripture passage can be made.

Bible study

All ages need to be learners of the Word. However, methods of studying the Bible vary with the age of the pupils. For spiritual growth to occur, both at-home preparation by the teacher and in-class participation by the pupil must create personal involvement with God's Word.

The story approach is one of the most effective ways to teach young children. Bible characters and events provide exciting story material. Children love Bible stories and enjoy memorizing portions from them. The amount children can learn should not be underestimated. They understand that the Bible is a true and special book about God and tells of people's obedience or disobedience to Him. Even a five-year-old can respond to the truth he hears by expressing his love for God or a desire to please Him.

Do you expect enough response from the young children you teach?

Young readers should also read some key Bible books, chapters, and verses on their own since familiarity with Scripture increases with use. Often, pupils' manuals provide Bible investigation methods to aid in this process.

Older pupils develop basic Bible skills as they learn the books of the Bible and find Scripture passages. They also can investigate historical background, geography, and customs. Besides such individual activities, group study provides meaningful opportunity to consider Bible truths as they apply to personal situations and current issues. Both research and problem-solving approaches effectively involve older pupils in Bible study.

What ways have you found to involve your pupils in Bible study?

Bible memorization

VBS encourages memorization of God's Word. Bible verses are usually an integral part of the lesson and a spirit of participation in the group makes memorization the normal activity. With review the next day, learning is reinforced. Bible memorization is not just for the children's department. Youth and adults also should be motivated to learn pertinent passages of Scripture. Young people might search out and memorize those promises of God which fit their own life situations. To help answer their friends' questions about God and the Bible as well as their own, adults should learn Scripture verses.

Those memorizing Scripture need to understand the meaning of the verses as well as the words. Comparing versions, looking up words in a dictionary, and discussing verse meaning help accomplish this.

Memory verses are an important part of the lesson and should capsulize key truths. Pupils can think through applications of the verses to their own lives. When memorization is an entire department endeavor with both teachers and pupils working together, the importance and relevance of passages is highlighted.

Awareness of pupil needs and abilities increases as the teacher clarifies any unusual words. By citing life situations and asking pupils to quote a verse which they could use in each situation, verses are made a natural part of the teaching scene.

There are numerous ways to teach Bible verses. Visual aids make memorization more interesting and help pupils visualize the passage. Learning activities such as puzzles, secret codes, dramatizations, and puppets stimulate enthusiasm to memorize. Tape recorders, songs, Bible drills, and recitation increase the diversity of approaches to Bible memorization.

"I will delight to do Thy will, O my God; Thy law is within my heart" (Ps. 40:8). "Thy word I have treasured in my heart, that I may not sin against Thee" (Ps. 119:11). It cannot be denied that changed lives will result from effective Bible study and meaningful Bible memorization.

Have you selected Bible memory portions which can be understood by the age level you are teaching?

CREATIVE TEACHING

A creative teacher will supplement and vary teaching methods since pupils learn in different ways and appreciate variety. Research, games, projects, dramatizations, and reports stimulate pupil interest, challenge teacher creativity, and help accomplish goals. Some bases for determining teaching methods for a particular lesson are the nature of the Bible content, the desired result of the lesson, the age and size of the group, and the facilities available.

Storytelling

Everyone loves a good story. Christ was a master storyteller. He captivated and convicted His hearers with parables and metaphors related to everyday experience.

A good story describes events naturally so that all listening enter into its experiences, thoughts, and actions, and are motivated to apply the spiritual truth to their own experience.

Every good story needs a beginning which sets the stage for action. The story then develops the action in an orderly fashion toward the climax. A life challenge should be evident so the conclusion is only long enough to account for the major characters and issues in the plot. Truth should be inherent in the story so no moralizing is necessary.

Thorough preparation is essential to effective storytelling. The speaker must become so absorbed in the story that its central message becomes real to listeners. A well prepared teacher has read the story aloud several times in order to present it naturally in his own words. Dialogue, action-packed words, and effective gestures add impact.

How can you prepare to tell a good story effectively?

Drama

Drama is a simple, natural expression of learning. Well planned dramatization goes beyond mere recall of facts to exploration of feelings. Pupils assume the role of another person, empathize with that person's feelings, and begin to understand why that person acted or reacted in a certain situation.

All enjoy drama—young children through adults. The degree of refinement and the spontaneity of the experience vary with the age group. A child's imagination is vivid so very few props are needed. To him, a chair *is* a throne; the tablecloth thrown over his shoulders *is* a Roman toga. Older groups may prefer costumes and more elaborate scenery. However, if emphasis shifts to details of production and away from feeling with the character, spontaneity may be lost. Actually, a well told story, enthusiastic pupils, and an ordinary room are all the ingredients necessary for effective drama.

Pupils need encouragement and guidance to express their ideas for acting out a story. The characters, situation, setting, and action must be decided.

Even though very young children cannot make their own drama decisions, they enjoy finger plays and rhymes. The actions of a story can be reviewed using finger or body motions. They delight in pretend situations. For example, everyone is baby Moses curled up in a basket, or everyone is walking along the road to see Jesus. Younger children also enjoy doing spontaneous pantomime of a Bible story they have just heard. It provides insight into the feelings of characters such as the sad lame man, the boy who willingly gave his lunch, the happy children going to see Jesus. It also gives opportunity for necessary movement.

Older pupils often desire more complex dramatization. Juniors, for example, prefer an action-packed plot with an interesting lead character involved in exciting activities. They recognize the importance of communicating a message worth remembering.

How have you learned from drama?

Audiovisuals

Audiovisuals both supplement and complement good teaching. Use them as a point of contact or in the summary or review to involve more of the pupils' senses. Each one should be well prepared and previewed or practiced in advance.

There are a variety of visual boards—chalk, bulletin, flannel, pocket, magnetic—on which to display pictures, words, and objects. Proper use of them creates an attractive teaching atmosphere. The pupils themselves can be involved in setting up and maintaining missionary or other displays during VBS. Pictures, charts, flash cards, and maps contribute to pupil understanding in ways words cannot accomplish. Posters and drawings can highlight Bible truth or a missionary emphasis. In addition, a mural may illustrate a Bible story or a continuous Bible theme.

Teaching aids such as films, filmstrips, slides, and overhead transparencies requiring equipment are known as projected materials. To effectively use films and filmstrips, a teacher can introduce key ideas and give pointers on important details to look for before showing the material. Discussion of these issues afterwards reveals what was gained by the pupils. Either small group interaction or large group discussion is beneficial in accomplishing this.

Slides and motion pictures help acquaint pupils with missionary work and other activities outside their experience or understanding. Use of the overhead projector is also valuable for visualizing words of songs, Bible verses, activity instructions, and pupil contributions.

Resources which involve listening also are effective. Records and cassettes, for instance, may set the room mood, introduce a new song, tell a story, and provide activity music for young children. Tape recorders can also capture pupil contributions.

The range of available teaching aids is immense. Puppets help re-tell stories and act out situations while providing much enjoyment. Moveable stand-up figures add interest to Bible stories. Models of biblical artifacts help pupils understand the life and times of Bible characters. In the same manner, a missionary who displays and explains some of his curios highlights the customs and life of a particular culture. When coupled with use of a globe or map to give pupils perspective on the location in relation to other countries, awareness of mission fields is greatly increased.

Field trips also enrich teaching. A trip to a local museum may be a real learning experience. Missionary projects can be personalized by visiting a children's home, hospital, convalescent home, or the home of a shut-in.

What aids are available in your church?

Music

Group singing, instrumental music, rhythm band, special music, and choral recitation provide a variety of music experiences. Since music involves the feelings, thoughts, and emotions of the learner, care should be exercised in choice. Songs should reinforce the theme or daily objective. Wording also is important. Is the vocabulary appropriate for and understandable by the age level? Can the song become the pupil's own expression? Songs suggested in the curriculum may require time and effort to learn, but pupils will be singing within their own voice range and life experience.

Do the songs chosen for your VBS meet these standards for music selection?

When teaching a new song, a teacher should sing through it once completely. Then visualize words on a chalkboard, flip chart, or overhead projector. Discuss the song's key thoughts and any difficult words or concepts. Having given this background, all should join in singing. The number of new songs used during VBS should be limited so that those learned can be sung frequently.

Use instrumental talent for more than accompaniment to group singing. Young children enjoy rhythm bands. Percussion instruments such as drums, triangles, tambourines, cymbals, and bells can be made or purchased inexpensively. Older pupils enjoy playing in a band, orchestra, or special music group to enrich the program.

Group choral reading provides the opportunity for meaningful reading of Scripture. With use of dynamics and rhythm, the power and beauty of its message become more evident.

SUMMARY

Teaching the Bible and involving pupils in meaningful Bible learning activities are the primary tasks of VBS. Bible study and Bible memorization guided by the teacher help the pupil discover God's truth and its application for his life. Personal preparation and continual spiritual growth equip the teacher to focus on pupils' needs, help them discover God's answer, and lead them in responding to the God of the Bible.

Use of a variety of methods enhances teaching/learning. To involve pupils in the lesson, teaching techniques should reflect creativity. Storytelling appeals to all ages and effectively communicates situations, actions, and characters. Drama, in addition to recalling facts, encourages pupils to explore the feelings of others.

Audiovisuals help pupils learn by involving more of the senses. In the same manner, well chosen and carefully taught music is a powerful teaching tool since the words will often be remembered long after VBS is completed.

FOR REVIEW

1. Suggest ways to involve pupils in Bible study.
2. List key principles to follow when leading pupils in Scripture memorization.
3. Identify various types of creative teaching.
4. Explain the role of audiovisuals in teaching a lesson.
5. Give guidelines for choosing and teaching songs in VBS.

FOR DISCUSSION

1. Interact with several class members and determine what is involved in the teaching/learning process.
2. Discuss methods which have been successfully used by class members to lead pupils in personal Bible discovery.
3. How can a teacher thoroughly prepare himself for Bible teaching in VBS?

FOR APPLICATION

1. Based on principles in this chapter, guide class members in memorizing a verse of Scripture or teach them a new song.
2. Prepare and tell a Bible story to a Sunday school class; report on your experience.

FOR ADDITIONAL ENRICHMENT

Barrett, Ethel. *Storytelling, It's Easy.* Grand Rapids: Zondervan, 1960.
Fulbright, Robert G. *New Dimensions in Teaching Children.* Nashville: Broadman Press, 1971.
Gangel, Kenneth O. *24 Ways to Improve Your Teaching.* Wheaton, IL: Victor Books, 1974.

Expressional Activities

9

Expressional activities reinforce lesson ideas, establish Bible truths, and clarify concepts. These activities allow pupils to share their feelings and respond to the truths of Scripture as they express the lesson creatively. Each activity should coordinate with the lesson aim as well as relate to pupil needs and abilities.

INDIVIDUAL / GROUP ACTIVITIES

Writing, art, and vocal activities can effectively involve pupils either individually or cooperatively. The continuous, concentrated length of VBS, however, provides rich opportunity for group interaction.

Written expression

Assignments in pupils' manuals help them investigate and recall facts from the Bible lesson. Questions, puzzles, acrostics, hidden names, and pictures often are used, depending on the age group. References to related passages of Scripture help pupils integrate Bible knowledge and discover meaning. Life-related illustrations and open-ended questions allow pupils to think through responses to Bible truths and apply them to their lives. The well prepared teacher guides pupils to investigate, integrate, and apply Scripture through personal assistance and encouragement. At the same time, the Holy Spirit guides each pupil to an understanding of the Word.

Notebooks can be an alternate or supplement to pupils' manuals, depending on the school's size, finances, and staff ability. Individually-made notebooks usually include factual information about the lesson and personal response to Bible truth in the form of a prayer, essay, questions, or artwork. Group or departmental notebooks with contributions from individuals or small groups can be made in much the same manner.

Pupils benefit when they rewrite lessons as a story, a first-person account, an interview, or a play. Creative writing of poems, stories, essays, letters, prayers, dramas, lyrics, and tunes allows personal expression of thoughts and feelings toward and about God. Often more openness can be expressed in written rather than verbal communication. Writing helps crystallize decisions captured on paper. Since writing can reveal thoughts and fears, love and encourage each pupil in his attempts to convey innermost feelings.

A daily or weekly school paper provides a unique opportunity for cooperative and creative effort. Students exercise their talents by submitting class or department news such as names of newcomers, birthdays, personal items, and words of songs and Bible verses to be learned.

Do you have forms of written expression included in lessons to encourage creativity?

Art expression

Items like crayons, chalk, paints, felt pens, clay, papier-mache, or plaster of Paris used with some imagination result in art expression. Most pupils enjoy working with one or more of these items to illustrate what they have learned and to express their emotions. Because art creation is uniquely one's own, pupils delight in displaying their work to classmates and to parents and friends at the closing activities.

Pupils of all ages enjoy drawing. This is an opportunity to represent Bible scenes, story action, and modern life situations on paper.

With group effort, a mural containing a series of pictures or one large more complex scene can be made. A cardboard box TV can be constructed by fastening miniature panels together, rolling the entire strip scroll-fashion onto two pieces of dowel or broom handle, cutting out a screen, and decorating the rest of the box. Then the TV is ready for pupils to turn the dowels and illustrate a story.

Pupils can make flannelgraph sets by covering a piece of heavy cardboard with flannel. To make the job easier, back with flannel and cut out small-scale figures drawn by the pupils or pictures from Sunday school papers. Encourage pupils to retell the VBS Bible stories with their flannelgraphs.

Map-making acquaints pupils with towns, rivers, lakes, and seas of missionary or Bible lands. It is possible to draw maps on overhead transparencies or use flannel-backed ones on flannelboards. Variety can be introduced by using salt-and-flour relief maps, sandtable maps, or papier-mache maps to illustrate geography. Maps pasted on heavy cardboard and cut apart like puzzles can be used for review.

Vocal expression

Pupils become more involved in class when they sense freedom to express their thoughts, ideas, and feelings. When they do, the teacher gains valuable insights into individual personalities and perspectives. Children gladly answer questions and share their ideas. Enthusiasm may divert the group, but the skillful teacher is able to maintain a lively discussion which centers around the lesson theme.

Question and answer sessions allow older pupils to verbalize truth comprehended and to clarify thinking. Yet, to arrive at a solution, discussion must go beyond the question-answer format to group interaction. A clearly defined problem, then, provides the key to good discussion and the opportunity to explore possible solutions in the light of God's Word.

Opportunities to retell stories, act them out in pantomine, or use flannelgraph, pictures, or costumes of Bible characters thrill many pupils. Older pupils enjoy recording Bible, missionary, or life-related stories on tape and then acting out scenes to the narration.

Role play, a spontaneous form of drama, allows pupils to assume roles of other persons to better understand them and the situations in which they are involved. This type of drama can explore emotions and attitudes and relate them to biblical principles. Often in role play a story situation is read or told up to the moment of climax. The class completes the story by assuming and playing out the different roles. To derive maximum benefit from role play, each player should take a few minutes to think about the feelings, speech, appearance, and actions of his role before beginning. The teacher should also alert the audience to look for the players' actions and reactions. When the players reach a solution, conclude the idea, or need additional information, the role play ends. If desired, the situation can be reenacted with other players. Following the role play, a group discussion and evaluation of the solution is beneficial. This is an excellent opportunity for the teacher to guide pupils toward living by biblical principles.

Different means of expressions should not be isolated from each other or be limited in their usage. A variety of creative combinations are possible. For instance, Bible stories, Bible verses, or lesson themes can be set to music and accompanied by musical instruments while pupils present a pantomine.

How can you create an atmosphere where pupils feel free to express their thoughts and feelings?

AROUND-THE-WORLD ACTIVITIES

Christ's Great Commission is the central point of Christian service. Vacation Bible School, therefore, emphasizes missions and world-wide outreach even as it reaches out into its own community. Helping pupils discover God's view of the world by providing information and challenging their involvement in meeting needs both near and far are both goals of an effective VBS missionary education program.

Although some curriculum supplies include missionary material, churches often personalize missions by featuring some of their own missionaries or mission areas. Selecting one area of missions and integrating it into each department program creates a unified impact throughout the school.

Information

To obtain information on a particular missions activity, a missionary might speak to the various departments. Planning ahead is necessary to secure missionaries home on furlough or in the area. Both home and foreign missions should be included for a well-rounded program.

Missionaries involved in VBS need information concerning how and when they are scheduled and specifics regarding age groups, time allotment, and special needs. If special equipment, such as slide projector, screen, or extension cord, is needed this should be provided. Housing and mealtime arrangements also may be necessary.

Special missionary emphasis may be accomplished through a missionary period, worship with a missions theme, Bible study on missions, Scripture memorization focusing on missions, or missionary songs. Having missionaries or Christians from other countries eat in the homes of different VBS pupils involves families in missions. Perhaps a Christian from another country could speak in some departments and broaden the view of missions by sharing from his own background. As he displays and demonstrates cultural artifacts, he acquaints pupils with life in another country and how Christianity relates to it.

If it is not possible for a missionary to attend VBS, alternative methods to foster missions can be used. Invite one of the church missionaries to send slides and a taped message describing his ministry. In addition, photos of missionary families and their work build interest. Candidates for the mission field or students returning from short-term mission work are also resources. When such contacts are unavailable, individual or group study helps pupils understand the missionary's life situation. Use as many sources as possible to learn about a particular country or area. To increase awareness of political and social current events, older pupils should watch the newspaper and magazines. Pupils can create posters, bulletin boards, and murals based on the information gathered. It would be helpful to provide practical details about mission boards, types of workers needed in different fields, educational preparations required, and the implications of current political scenes with regard to missions.

Flannelgraph and flash card missionary stories also provide missions information. A single lesson or a series can depict the culture of a country, needs of the people, missionaries serving there and their work. Missionary story books, biographies, research, skits, and plays further enrich the VBS missions program.

How will your missions emphasis be informative?

Involvement

Pupils will long remember those activities in which they feel personally involved. If a missionary shares some of his background, how God called him for mission service, or current prayer requests/answers, pupils feel closer to him. The more interaction that takes place between missionary and pupils during VBS, the greater the prayer support and other involvement later. Pupils may make a tape or write letters to newfound friends on the mission field after VBS is completed.

Using offerings to fund special mission projects is a unique feature of VBS. Pupil interest and enthusiasm are stimulated when a particular need is recognized. It may be personal such as a typewriter, slide projector, battery-operated amplifier. It may be a field need such as bricks for building or pulpit furniture. A home missionary may suggest buying new clothes for migrant families or Bibles for home Bible study groups.

Personal contact, prayer, and project participation are key ways to involve pupils in missions. Teachers should also be prepared to help pupils commit their lives to a special ministry for the Lord.

What opportunities for missionary involvement are possible in your program?

HANDCRAFT ACTIVITIES

Crafts are a popular feature of VBS since pupils can apply concepts learned in class in a creative and enjoyable manner. Whether the VBS staff develops its own craft activities, follows curriculum suggestions, or buys ready-made kits, several criteria are helpful when deciding upon handcrafts. A correlation between crafts and the VBS theme should be evident. At the same time, craft activities need to fit the abilities of each age group so that pupils are able to do them individually. Costly and time-consuming crafts are not necessary for effectiveness.

When handcraft activities are decided, each worker in the department should prepare a sample—even if there is a craft director—so he will be able to assist pupils. The process of working on the craft is as important as the product since biblical principles are being taught. Sufficient supplies, equipment, and work space with adequate time for proper cleanup are essential ingredients for an effective handcraft time.

How do your handcraft activities draw attention to biblical principles?

ADVENTURES IN SERVICE

The church, home, and community provide opportunities to practice biblical principles. Grounds work, repainting, repairing toys and furniture, making curtains, or preparing bulletin boards are possible ways to help improve church facilities. Before beginning any project, though, approval should be secured from the board and arrangements made with the custodian. Appreciation and service can be expressed to parents by doing the dishes, running errands cheerfully without pay, straightening the bedroom without being told, cleaning the garage, or mowing the lawn.

Community projects vary with area needs and the age of pupils. Visitation at a convalescent home, a hospital, or the homes of shut-ins to present a brief program of songs and Bible drama is possible. Favors for invalid trays, cards or letters to the sick, flowers or toys can be prepared in advance to take along. In addition, time might be spent chatting or helping with tasks. Older pupils could spend a day helping with repairs and cleanup at a gospel mission or going in witnessing teams to a park or shopping center. The possibilities for service are limited only by recognition of needs and the time available to fill them.

Do the service opportunities planned for your VBS appeal to your pupils?

SUMMARY

Expressional activities not only reinforce lesson concepts but also provide outlets for pupils to respond to Bible truth. Individual and group activities directly related to the theme of the day which arise out of the Bible story or Bible study may have written, art, or vocal expression. Around-the-world activities focus on information about mission areas and missionaries as well as involvement with them through personal contact, prayer, and special projects. Handcraft activities can be an integral part of the curriculum or simply supplement the theme. Service activities provide opportunities in the church, home, or community to practice biblical truths. When pupils are doing as well as listening, their vision broadens. As they participate in enriching experiences, the VBS ministry expands in a dynamic manner.

FOR REVIEW

1. How do expressional activities aid learning?
2. List the various expressional forms and tell the values of each.
3. Suggest several ways pupils can engage in individual and group activities.
4. Identify the two major goals of missionary education and list several ways to achieve them.
5. How can involvement in service activities become a natural result of VBS teaching/learning?

FOR DISCUSSION

1. In what ways will missions emphasis vary according to age groups?
2. What is the value of handcraft activities?
3. How do service projects provide opportunity for expressing Bible teaching?

FOR APPLICATION

1. Interview at least five people who have been VBS pupils. Discover what handcrafts were most meaningful and whether they still have some crafts made in VBS.
2. Write a missionary or missions society for suggestions on how missions can be presented in VBS.

FOR ADDITIONAL ENRICHMENT

Beegel, Shirley, ed. *Creative Craft Ideas For All Ages.* Cincinnati: Standard Publishing Co., 1966.
Doan, Eleanor. *More Handcrafts And Fun.* Grand Rapids: Zondervan, 1966.

Recreational Activities

10

Recreation, the renewal of mental and physical well-being, is essential to the development of the total person. The manner in which this need is met influences the attitudes of pupils toward life interpersonal relationships.

VALUES OF RECREATION

Recreation refreshes and restores body and mind. When effectively planned, it is an integral part of the total teaching/learning experience of VBS.

Opportunity for fellowship

VBS provides the added dimension of Christian fellowship to social relationships. Informal, spirited interaction during recreation promotes fellowship. Opportunities for cooperative play not only offer fun and enjoyment, but also help teach norms of Christian living and social behavior.

Older children often enjoy competitive play such as team games and relay races. Competition is unhealthy, though, when winning becomes so important that the less skilled children are discriminated against. The recreation leader must select competitive activities with care so as to teach Christian values and to promote positive relationships.

Do the recreational activities selected for your VBS lead to cooperation or competition?

Practice Christian values

Play activities offer experiences in living. A primary consideration of the recreation leader should be the development of Christian character. Pupils begin to understand and experience some of the abstract concepts taught in the classroom through recreation. While people often verbalize their ideas about God and Christian relationships, practicing such concepts is more difficult. A demonstration of Christian principles by teachers both inside and outside the classroom helps pupils apply them.

How is Christian character being developed through recreational activities in your VBS?

Revitalize energies

A balance between study and play must be maintained for pupils to learn effectively. An extended period of sitting and concentration results in tired muscles and minds unless there are breaks for activity and movement. Children particularly need recreation since growing muscles require stretching, moving, and running to increase coordination. In addition, the short attention span of children requires changes in routine. Youth and adults also appreciate the opportunity to relax during a break.

PRINCIPLES OF RECREATION

When play is viewed as an important element in learning, the greatest benefit from recreational activities results. Leaders, participants, and activities should focus on how recreation can contribute to learning.

Leadership

Those leading recreation need to understand its purpose. If recreation is regarded as a time for pupils to run wildly and tire themselves or as a time of intense competition, valuable teaching/learning experiences are wasted. Instead, recreation should involve both pupils and teachers in a situation where biblical principles can be practiced. What potential recreation provides for reinforcing Christian development!

The leader also needs to know how to guide pupils in the game or activity chosen so all will enjoy it. Basic rules should be understood and conveyed to the pupils. Technical details of the game need to be explained sufficiently so that participants can enter fully into the activity without interruptions for clarification of rules.

Proper supervision is vital to effective recreation. Well trained and well prepared leadership fosters cooperation while it promotes group enjoyment.

Participants

Since activities are influenced by the people involved, awareness of characteristics, needs, interests, and abilities helps determine the recreation best suited for each age group. Discouragement and frustration may result when activities mismatch the comprehension or skills of a group. Therefore, curriculum materials usually suggest appropriate recreation for each age level. Various resources are available as well through a bookstore or community library. If more help is needed, an experienced school teacher may be able to recommend popular games.

The recreation leader should try to involve everyone in the activity without coercion. Choose activities enjoyed by most pupils of an age level. If a pupil refuses to participate, try to determine the reason. Competitive pressure may be so intense that the less talented pupils withdraw from needed physical activity. Are the rules clear? Would regrouping provide the security of friends? What is the pupil's attitude?

Encourage each pupil to take part, but be prepared to minister to the spectator with a positive, loving attitude.

Christians should be alert to reach out in true love and concern to those who are on the edge of the group. A friendly word, smile, or gesture may encourage them to become involved.

Are your VBS recreation activities appropriate for the age level and interests of pupils?

Program

Recreation can meet many pupil needs if activities correlate with the VBS theme in an appropriate manner for the age of the participants. Cooperative team games rather than highly competitive sports should be emphasized. The activities should provide variety throughout the week and balance between active and quiet games so that pupils are not overstimulated physically or emotionally. Weather will influence the choice of games. Plan alternative activities for bad weather keeping in mind the space which is available. At times, recreation which can take place within the department or classroom area is a refreshing change.

To maximize use of facilities and staff, correlate departmental schedules. Depending on the size of the recreation area, it may be best to have only one or two departments involved at a time. It is essential to schedule sufficient time for the activities planned as well as time for washroom and drinking fountain visits.

To obtain adequate space, it may be necessary to rope off a section of the parking lot, set boundaries on the church lawn, or use a nearby school athletic field or park playground. If several areas are designated for recreation, each department should be aware of its space. Adequate and easily accessible supplies also should be ready for use.

Attention to such program details assures the greatest benefits from recreation time. When advance planning is handled with care, little time is wasted and the total recreational period can be enjoyable and satisfying for both teacher and pupil.

Is maximum use of recreation time being made in your department?

TYPES OF RECREATION

Recreation encompasses more than just games. While outdoor events like sports, camping, and nature hikes are important, social gatherings such as parties and picnics also should be considered. Recreation also includes some of the expressional activities that take place within the departmental setting and are directly correlated with the lesson theme such as drama, literature, storytelling, arts and crafts, and hobbies. Chapters 8 and 9 provide details concerning these.

Essential activities

Whenever possible, play activities should take place outdoors. Toddlers enjoy riding activities to use up some of their energy. If mothers are willing to bring tricycles or wagons to VBS for their children, a section of the parking lot, gym, or all-purpose room should be roped off for them. Games with repetition, singing, circle activities, and pretend games are favorites with young children. Older children, in contrast, like low-key competition, team activities, and more complicated games. Modified versions of the activities can be used indoors.

To add variety use icebreakers; musical chairs; and guessing, table, and written games. Young children enjoy playing in a rhythm band, marching and singing to music, and active motion songs.

Nursery and kindergarten children require frequent changes of pace from activity to rest. Upon return from recreation, invite them to stretch out on a carpet or mats. With dim lights and quiet music, read a short simple story correlated with the lesson while they relax. This will soothe overactive, excited children and establish a more reverent mood. Older children can sit quietly or rest heads and arms on a table while soft music plays or a story is told.

Does your department vary activities?

Refreshments are a welcome treat for VBS pupils. Simple, inexpensive combinations of fruit juice, milk, or ade mixtures and cookies, crackers, or pretzels are enjoyed. As a special treat, ice cream cups might be served.

With younger children, it is often more convenient to serve refreshments in the room while they are seated at tables. If this is done, they can wait until everyone is served and thank God for the food. Older children may prefer having refreshments near the kitchen or outdoors. Thanks may be given before they leave their classroom or group activity. Adults enjoy either a cold beverage, coffee, or tea with a cookie or pastry. The entire church can help provide refreshments as a service to VBS.

Extra features

Special activities are welcome events during VBS even though they require extra time and effort. A two-week school may feature an event such as a picnic or a party at the end of the first week to build enthusiasm and morale for the following week. Or, to climax the fellowship experienced throughout VBS, a closing picnic or party can be held.

For any and all activities decided upon, every detail must be carefully planned. Those who will attend, arrangements for food, location and transportation details, plans for recreation and cleanup, and the responsibilities of each teacher and helper must be considered carefully.

For a successful picnic, encourage the entire student body and faculty to attend. A nearby park or farm appeals to pupils and simplifies transportation. Activities for all ages should move rapidly once they are underway so that the picnic does not last too long. A time of singing, sharing, and giving testimonies is a meaningful way to conclude.

Alternative closing day special treats might include cake, cupcakes, ice cream, or an unusual refreshment treat in each department. Older pupils may plan a picnic lunch. A trip or outing which relates to the theme could be part of the VBS program and greatly enrich studies. Older pupils have the maturity and interest to benefit from special outings while they enjoy the change of routine.

What special activities are you considering for your pupils?

Teachers as well as pupils enjoy social events. A kick-off banquet or luncheon for the staff encourages unity. Informal times of fellowship with the entire staff also are helpful. Otherwise it is easy for teachers to become completely involved in activities of only one department. It is interesting how much refreshments boost the morale and encourage interaction at staff meetings. A refreshment break during the recreation period provides another opportunity for a portion of the staff to interact. This is possible if recreation responsibilities are rotated. A reception at the close of VBS to show appreciation for the staff's work is another possibility.

What kinds of social fellowship will be provided for VBS teachers in your church?

SUMMARY

Needs of the total person must be recognized. With proper guidance, VBS recreational activities can meet many of the social, spiritual, emotional, mental, and physical needs of pupils. "Jesus kept increasing in wisdom and stature, and in favor with God and men" (Luke 2:52). So may VBS participants.

Recreation provides opportunities for fellowship and practice of Christian values besides a physical outlet for energy. Both organization and supervision of this time by qualified leaders are essential if full participation and learning are to result from the program. Including a variety of age-appropriate activities that correlate with the VBS theme increases benefits. These activities should have enough flexibility that necessary changes do not disrupt the program.

Recreation is not limited to games. Sporting events, social gatherings, and expressional activities are included. When weather permits, use of the outdoors often is preferred for recreation.

To supplement the usual recreation program, extra features might be added at various times during VBS. Whatever activities are selected, they should help bring pupils, parents, VBS staff, and the congregation closer together.

FOR REVIEW

1. What are some values of recreation?
2. How does leadership contribute to effective recreation?
3. What considerations of the participants influence recreation plans and procedures?
4. List some essential recreational activities.
5. What activities can be planned as extra features of VBS?

FOR DISCUSSION

1. What do you consider a biblical view of recreation? How does this influence the choice of VBS activities?
2. What is the proper balance between study and play in VBS?
3. How can VBS meet the needs of the enthusiastic pupil as well as the spectator through the recreation program?

FOR APPLICATION

1. Plan recreational activities for a VBS keeping in mind basic principles for good recreation.
2. Decide upon a social event for the final day of VBS that will strengthen ties with the church and Sunday school and promote maximum enjoyment and participation. Plan some of the details.

FOR ADDITIONAL ENRICHMENT

Keeler, Ronald F. *Games for Children*. Cincinnati: Standard Publishing, 1967.

Solving Problems

11

People work closely together in VBS, frequently in less-than-ideal situations, and problems can easily arise. Busy schedules leave little time to solve them. However, advance planning, preparation, and prayer prevent many problems. When leaders and committees plan together, some problem areas can be foreseen and alternate procedures arranged.

Seeking the Lord's guidance and blessing upon VBS is a natural part of church life. The entire church family needs to uphold teachers, pupils, and program before the Lord. For the most part, administrative problems can be worked out long before VBS begins, but difficulties with pupils are less predictable. Attendance, absenteeism, and behavior problems are unknown factors to be prayed about even before VBS begins. Problems that arise in these areas must be dealt with promptly and effectively.

Have possible problems been considered in your department?

ATTENDANCE

VBS exists for pupils. Pupils must be attracted to and involve themselves in VBS for their needs and interests to be met.

Promotion, personal contact, pre-registration, and prayer encourage pupil attendance. While an attractive, personalized invitation saturated with prayer can move hearts to respond, the decision to attend rests with each pupil and his parents. Once pupils enroll, responsibility for continuing attendance is shared by the teacher.

Encourage attendance

The teacher's personality and attitudes play a vital role in attendance patterns. Since VBS is brief, it is important that the teacher establish warm personal relationships from the first day. Learn pupils' names and individual interests as quickly as possible. Those who sense friendship and concern will want to return. Opportunities to talk about topics of importance to pupils encourage attendance. Personal rapport also enables the teacher to gain insights about the individual and the teaching/learning situation. Informal moments during pre-session, recreation, refreshment break, and craft time are opportunities to get better acquainted. These times may prove to be more valuable than any other contact to reach pupils spiritually as well as to encourage attendance.

How do you get acquainted with your pupils?

Involving pupils in a well planned daily program to discover God's truth helps stabilize attendance. If pupils see how each day's knowledge contributes to the next, the importance of consistent participation will be recognized. The more relevant Bible stories and Bible studies are to the pupils, the greater the motivation to attend. Projects, special assignments, and crafts that take several days to complete bring pupils back.

Assigning responsibilities also helps pupils become involved. Children, for example, generally want to help arrange tables and chairs, distribute and put away supplies, serve refreshments, operate audiovisual equipment, lead in prayer, and run errands. For youth, work on a group service project helps them become part of the group while they serve others.

The program itself should attract pupils. Appealing workbooks and craft projects as well as activities appropriate to interest and ability help create and maintain enthusiasm. Pupils respond to a program that moves from one activity to another quickly enough to maintain interest yet without a sense of being rushed. Music and special features such as missions emphasis and service projects help accomplish this.

Besides the intrinsic motivation to attend VBS because of good teacher-pupil relationships and effective teaching, extra incentives may be offered. Bible verse cards, attendance charts and certificates, and other visuals promote attendance while providing a continuing record.

Contests are effective whether they are inter-class, inter-department, or based on individual achievement. When promoting a contest, care should be taken that the contest remains an incentive and does not become an end in itself. The inner satisfaction of having excellent attendance should be rewarding. Offering bigger and better awards each year must be avoided if contests are to remain in proper perspective.

One problem with contests is that some must lose. It is difficult to assess the time and effort each pupil or team puts into a contest, especially when each one feels that he tried his best. Rewards, therefore, in VBS should recognize everyone's efforts. A picnic or a special treat for all accomplishes this purpose.

Are the time and effort of pupils who attend VBS recognized?

Absenteeism and tardiness

In spite of good teaching, teacher-pupil relationships, and program planning, some absenteeism will occur. A pupil may find it difficult to relate to VBS because the program is new and strange to him, or he may feel ill at ease among unfamiliar people. Home situations such as the family vacation, illness, oversleeping, responsibilities, or punishment for misbehavior may prevent attendance. At times, scheduled events like music or swimming lessons, community programs, or a doctor's appointment may preempt VBS attendance.

Regardless of the reason, the teacher should make every effort to contact the absent pupil and encourage attendance. A follow-up system in which the secretary submits the list of absentees to teachers or callers who, in turn, contact pupils usually works well. Often, a visit or phone call is more effective than mailing a card since VBS is so brief. In addition, direct communication with the pupil and parent helps the caller ascertain why the pupil was absent. He also has opportunity to personally express interest in the pupil and encourage his attendance the next day. These personal contacts make later follow-up visits easier and promote good home-church relationships.

Starting VBS promptly with an interest-catcher usually discourages tardiness. An on-time space may be included on attendance records so that those who are punctual may be recognized at the closing program. When tardiness is habitual, it may be due to the home situation. A phone call clarifies starting time procedures and informs the parent of what the pupil is missing by not being on time.

DISCIPLINE

Often discipline is thought of as punishment done *to* a child when he misbehaves. Actually, discipline is something that is done *for* and *with* a child. Discipline is training which corrects and guides the individual as he progresses from external control by parents, teachers, adults, and older children to self-control and guidance by the Holy Spirit. Some pupils require a great deal of external control to benefit from group experiences while others have reached a point of fairly reliable self-control and can function happily within a looser framework. The VBS teacher should attempt to identify causes for misbehavior and seek ways to encourage positive actions that help pupils develop into Spirit-guided, self-controlled individuals.

Identify causes for misbehavior

While a pupil may not know why he acts the way he does, the teacher needs to attempt to identify the cause. First, the teacher must examine his attitudes toward his pupils, particularly those that misbehave. He should also evaluate the degree to which his teaching is spiritually prepared, relevant to needs, and exemplified by his life-style.

In the classroom, check whether improper seating, unnecessary distractions, or inadequate supplies impede the creation of an environment where pupils know each other and interact in a happy, friendly atmosphere.

Consider elements in the pupil's home environment which might make him seek special attention. It may be that a permissive atmosphere at home prevails so the pupil has difficulty controlling himself in a group. Those actions which seem unacceptable at VBS may result from expressions of speech, habits, apathy, or a lack of reverence that are found in the home.

Finally, study the pupil to see how he reacts in group situations. His actions may be done out of thoughtlessness, to gain attention, or to express boredom with materials that lack challenge. Whatever the case, the pupil needs an extra portion of love and understanding.

The circumstances and pupils involved in each problem situation must be examined as objectively as possible. When this is done, causes of the problem can often be alleviated or completely removed. Indeed, the maxim "There is no such thing as a problem child; there is only a child with a problem" has validity.

Encourage positive behavior

To set the proper atmosphere for good behavior, expect positive behavior and commend it when it is present. At the same time, establish authority kindly but firmly from the start. Once the entire staff or department agrees upon boundaries of discipline, each teacher should set and explain ground rules to his class. The number of rules should be limited to avoid confusing and frustrating pupils. In some cases, pupils may even formulate their own rules. In any event, teachers should work together as a team to maintain positive behavior.

Has your staff or department decided upon boundaries of discipline?

When problems are handled lovingly but firmly, pupils sense genuine concern. Love promotes positive behavior and satisfies pupils' needs. Prayer for God's guidance and blessing upon every decision is also an essential ingredient in discipline.

Many problem situations can be avoided if the lesson is thoroughly prepared so the teacher is able to devote attention to the pupils' reactions. The program should move quickly and change pace when restlessness occurs. Workers should interact with pupils during both study and recreation activities. By sitting with the pupils, workers can actively participate and also direct attention to the one leading the group. Many seating arrangement problems disappear when adults are seated among the pupils.

The staff should not only decide rules, but also help enforce them. Each teacher needs to deal with problems as soon as possible. Speak to misbehavers individually about the behavior and consequences that will result when rules are not obeyed. While assuring the offender of a willingness to help, challenge him to more positive behavior. Sometimes an agreed-upon signal such as a wink or a nod of the head reminds the pupil to practice good behavior. When disobedience does occur, disciplinary measures must be carried out promptly.

How often does your staff meet to pray for individual pupils?

Anticipate challenging situations

When an unusually large enrollment results in an unrealistic teacher-pupil ratio, reorganization is necessary. Capitalize on the desire of most older pupils to help themselves, and encourage them to do as much as possible before seeking assistance. Cooperative efforts of small groups and teamwork should be praised. With younger children, it is essential to locate additional helpers when enrollment is too large. Some teenagers or mothers may volunteer their services on a rotating basis.

Occasionally a child will cry and no amount of comforting seems to help. The parent and teacher should agree on a plan of action if the child should continue to cry.

If an illness or accident occurs during VBS, immediately contact the parent to pick up the child. A teacher or worker may wish to accompany them to a doctor or a hospital emergency room in urgent cases, but the parent must decide upon the nature of the treatment.

The exceptionally bright pupil, the slow learner, the mentally or physically handicapped child may require special attention. Whenever possible, place a pupil in a group comparable to his school grouping. A mentally handicapped youngster, depending on the severity of his retardation, may function adequately within a normal grade group if the class is small enough for him to receive additional help. A teacher or other pupils may assist a physically handicapped pupil move from activity to activity.

Is your VBS able to meet the needs of a mentally or physically handicapped pupil?

Some pupils start attending VBS several days after the opening. Welcome late enrollees and try to assign a worker or an advanced pupil to help them catch up. Some may want to complete missed lessons at home. Teachers also may send home handwork from previous days for parents to work on with younger children.

People and problems seem to go together, but the promise of the Lord is with the teacher who faithfully ministers in VBS. "Then the word of the Lord came to Jeremiah, saying, 'Behold, I am the Lord, the God of all flesh; is anything too difficult for Me?' " (Jer. 32:26,27).

SUMMARY

Careful planning and preparation help a teacher avoid most problems which may arise in VBS. Difficulties with pupil attendance and behavior, though, are not predictable. Still, the teacher can do much to create a classroom atmosphere which discourages problems.

Daily attendance is promoted by the teacher's personal love and concern, pupil involvement, effective programming, and occasional extra incentives. Absentees should be contacted personally and encouraged to return. Starting VBS promptly with an interesting opener discourages tardiness.

Discipline should help move the pupil from external controls to self-control and guidance by the Holy Spirit. Identifying the causes for misbehavior helps a teacher develop a framework for favorable behavior. Positive expectations, love, and staff teamwork contribute to this framework. An unbalanced teacher-pupil ratio, illness and accidents, exceptional pupils, and late enrollees are additional areas which require consideration.

FOR REVIEW

1. Identify methods for encouraging attendance.
2. State several reasons for absenteeism.
3. Give at least three possible causes for misbehavior.
4. How can positive behavior be encouraged?
5. Name three challenging situations that can arise.

FOR DISCUSSION

1. How can VBS develop self-discipline in pupils?
2. What is the relationship of leadership characteristics to behavioral problems?
3. Use open-ended stories or role play to illustrate discipline problems, and then discuss possible solutions.

FOR APPLICATION

1. Prepare a list of useful contests for VBS based on suggestions in books, supply catalogs, or VBS materials.
2. Compare VBS attendance records in at least three schools. Seek to determine what each school did to encourage attendance and whether there is a pattern of attendance.

FOR ADDITIONAL ENRICHMENT

Dobson, James. *Dare to Discipline.* Wheaton, IL: Tyndale House Publishers, 1970.

Lasting Results

VBS is never over for results continue throughout the year. Commitments made to Jesus Christ during VBS will be put to the test of everyday living. Faithful prayer and nurturing are needed to maintain the growth process. Workers challenged and encouraged through VBS can use their gifts to edify the church in other ministries. VBS, often the beginning of new life and new experiences, extends its influence into the entire church year.

DECISIONS FOR CHRIST

If VBS is thoughtfully planned, faithfully administered, and prayerfully supported, pupils are confronted with the claims of Christ. In response to the gospel, some accept Christ as Savior, some make new strides in Christian growth, and some indicate concern for Christian service.

Lead pupils to Christ

During VBS the staff has opportunities to be used of God in winning pupils of all ages to Jesus Christ. "God so loved the world that He gave His only begotten Son, that whoever believes in Him should not perish, but have eternal life" (John 3:16). The Christian teacher also must love each pupil and sincerely endeavor to win him to Christ.

Teachers need a spiritual sensitivity to pupils. This increases with effort to become acquainted. A pupil may indicate that he has not received Christ. With this awareness of need for salvation or other problems, teachers can pray specifically for their pupils.

At an opportune time, the way of salvation can be clearly explained. Words and phrases understood by the age group must be used. Often the teacher's manual provides excellent guidelines for accomplishing this.

Pupils are helped to experience the reality of the person of Jesus Christ through Bible stories, lessons, verses, and personal life modeling. The pupil who makes a salvation decision with this background will comprehend more fully that he is committing his life to a person, the very Son of God.

Opportunities for response should be a natural part of the Bible lesson, the pupil's manual time, missionary emphasis, worship time, even casual conversations. While the timing may vary, often initiative will come from the pupil. Avoid emotional appeals or suggestion of reward, such as the offer of a free book, to elicit response. Speak to each one who wants to make a decision to determine the motivation behind the response. Making a decision is an important step. The pupil needs to think through his decision, talk about it, and pray with the one who guided him to this point. In this one-to-one relationship, questions and misunderstanding can be clarified.

Let the pupil pray in his own words. If he cannot, he may not be ready to make a decision, or he may not know how to pray aloud. Rather than give him words to repeat, let him talk about what he is doing and what he will say to God. Then let him pray these thoughts in his own words.

It is not possible to teach all there is to know about salvation and Christian living in a few brief moments. Help the pupil mark and read some key salvation verses in his Bible for future reference. Although using the Bible may be new and strange to some, a few verses lightly underlined with pencil can be ready references when assurance of salvation is needed.

Each decision requires careful follow-up. Every new Christian needs spiritual nurture. Follow-up suggestions are considered later in this chapter.

Could you comfortably talk with a pupil who wants to receive Christ as his Savior?

Guide in growth

Salvation is the first step in the adventure of living for Jesus Christ. VBS can help pupils also take succeeding steps in Christian maturity. Paul prayed that believers might "walk in a manner worthy of the Lord and to please Him in all respects, bearing fruit in every good work and increasing in the knowledge of God" (Col. 1:10). The Christian teacher also should pray this for his pupils who receive Christ.

Some pupils will make new commitments to Jesus Christ during VBS. A pertinent Bible lesson may cause some to confess sin in their lives. Pupils also may be convicted to read God's Word and pray regularly, to get involved in church and/or Sunday school, or to demonstrate Christ's love at home. To seal the new commitment, the teacher can talk and pray with the pupil privately as well as help him locate and mark some verses which promise God's power to enable him in his decision.

Develop for service

In response to the missionary emphasis, some pupils may dedicate their lives to full-time Christian ministry. The pastor or a missionary will want to spend time counseling these. Others may recognize the need to be better witnesses by life and word in their homes, neighborhoods, and schools and should be given help in witnessing to family and friends. In addition, the teacher can support the pupil's stepping out for God by telling of his availability to counsel and willingness to pray.

CLOSING PROGRAM

A brief, interesting, enjoyable, and Christ-honoring closing program is a fitting climax to VBS activities. Its major emphasis should be on relationships between teachers and pupils, teachers and parents, church and home rather than on performance.

Purpose

The closing event provides an excellent opportunity for teachers to meet parents and share some of the academic and spiritual accomplishments achieved by the children. Christian parents will thrill to evidences of growth while unchurched parents may ask questions about biblical teaching or spiritual matters. The friendly, genuinely Christian teacher can use these opportunities to open homes for further contact.

Along with informal opportunities to present Christ, the program itself provides a more formal method of presenting the gospel message. Christ and His love should be presented, explained, and demonstrated in a variety of ways by pupils who attended VBS.

Finally, the closing event provides a bridge between VBS and year-round ministries of the church. It can be shown that VBS is more than a brief, fun-filled activity; it is one of the church's many expressions of concern for families, children, youth, and adults. Involvement in other ministries of the church helps maintain the spiritual education begun in VBS.

Will your closing program build relationships?

Time and place

The closing program may take a variety of forms. It can be scheduled for the evening before the last day, the afternoon or evening of the last day, the Sunday evening service following the last day of VBS, or the regularly scheduled midweek service.

The church sanctuary, fellowship hall, or gym are suitable places to hold a closing program. Weather permitting, a lawn service impressively alerts the neighborhood to the church's ministry.

The program should be limited to 60-75 minutes to avoid restlessness. Well planned presentations that move smoothly and quickly are greatly appreciated by all.

Preparation

While the role and time allotment of each department, seating arrangements, and procedures for moving to and from the platform are overall planning decisions, most details are arranged on a departmental level. Suggestions for presentations usually are available in the curriculum.

Each department should meet early to plan its part in the program, a display of handcrafts, and ways to relate to parents who visit the department after the program. A short time should be spent on the last two days of VBS rehearsing the department presentation with the pupils.

After each department completes its plans, the VBS director coordinates the program. Copies distributed to the department superintendents several days before the program will eliminate confusion. Since the closing program emphasizes relationships rather than performance, rehearsals might be limited to departments.

Elements

Presentations of daily accomplishments, a pantomime of a Bible story to an oral or taped narration, songs, creative uses of Scripture, or a slide-tape presentation of VBS activities are possible elements in a closing program. If awards are to be presented and recognition given during the program, careful scheduling is necessary. To conserve time, have groups of pupils rather than individuals stand to be recognized for perfect attendance, punctuality, Bible memorization, and other honors. Presenting certificates in the departments after the program is finished also saves time. Teachers and committees can be recognized by groups as well, but time should be taken to express appreciation to the VBS director individually.

Pupils might present information on the missionary project to illustrate what they have learned and what they have accomplished. Visuals, a skit, or an interview could be used effectively. If the missionary involved is present, a special representation of the project given to him would be meaningful. If desired, brief testimonies by some who made decisions during VBS could be another feature in the program.

While the message of salvation should be inherent in department presentations, the pastor may wish to clarify the message and purpose of VBS as he expresses his own appreciation of the school. Then parents may visit displays of craft projects, pupils' books, and other items. Refreshments can be provided in the departments or in a central location. This is a time for church families to be sensitive and friendly to unchurched families.

A variation on the all-school program might be to hold an open house where pupils participate in a condensed edition of their normal day while parents move from room to room. Each department could plan a brief presentation in its own room.

FOLLOW-UP

Details involved in follow-up should be decided upon before VBS begins so that plans can be put into action immediately after the school closes.

Personal follow-up of pupils who made decisions helps insure growth in their Christian lives. A visit to the home of a pupil who made a decision for Christ is essential, particularly if he is young and does not know how to explain to his parents what has taken place in his life. This is an opportunity for another adult to explain the plan of salvation as well as what happened in the child's life. Encourage the parents to help their child grow in his new experience, and invite the family to attend Sunday school and church if they do not already do so.

Providing helpful booklets, tracts, Scripture memorization plans, Bible reading guides, and devotional books gives new Christians extra support and guidance.

Pupils of church families should share with their Sunday school teachers any decisions they make. In addition, the VBS teacher can alert the Sunday school teacher of this new step.

For the unchurched pupils who make decisions, the aim of follow-up should be evangelization of the entire family. It is easier for a pupil to continue in his newfound faith if his family is reached for Christ, and he feels their support. Unchurched families should be a continual prayer and personal contact concern of the church.

New workers who have made a meaningful service contribution

should be followed up also. They may be ready to assume some responsibility in the total church program, or they may need to develop their gifts further through training classes. The Christian education committee should interview such workers and explore their role in the ministry of the church.

Is a follow-up procedure planned for your VBS?

EVALUATION

Evaluation of VBS results is the final step in the process which began with setting goals. From those goals the program was determined, personnel recruited and trained, methods and materials provided, and VBS begun. What actually happened in each of these steps is determined by evaluation.

Facts must be gathered and put into final form. Compile in one report the enrollment and attendance figures of pupils and staff for each department. Information concerning finances, transportation, equipment, and supplies should be finalized.

On a more personal level, a complete list of staff with department and position, address and phone number, and a similar list for pupils by families should be compiled. The number and types of decisions made with recommendations for appropriate follow-up should be included. Prospects for decision follow-up, family visitation, and new worker contact should be sent to the proper agencies in the church.

Within two weeks following the close of VBS, the staff and planning committee should meet together for evaluation. Questionnaires may be distributed to the staff on the last day of VBS to be returned immediately or brought to the evaluation meeting.

Questions concerning department and overall goals and the degree to which they were met should be included. Evaluate the suitability of curriculum in meeting pupil needs. The adequacy of supplies, equipment, craft projects, and resources for effective teaching should be judged. In addition, considerations concerning the ability and availability of personnel, scheduling of activities, and areas in need of improvement is necessary. Information compiled from the completed questionnaires should be filed for next year's planning committee and director so that an even more effective ministry can be developed.

Was last year's evaluation used to determine this year's VBS program?

SUMMARY

As decisions made by pupils are acted upon, the results of VBS continue throughout the year. The teacher seeks to guide pupils, to experience the reality of the person of Jesus Christ and obedience to His Word. The quantity and quality of decisions themselves are indicators of the effectiveness of VBS.

The VBS closing program reflects what the pupils have achieved both academically and spiritually. It also provides opportunity for teachers to meet parents and invite them to become involved in the year-round ministry of the church.

Follow-up consists of contacting pupils who made decisions, new and unchurched families, and prospective workers. The methods to be used should be decided prior to the opening of VBS so they can begin immediately after the school closes.

Evaluation based on facts gathered from records, reports, and staff questionnaires must be completed soon after VBS ends. The extent to which the objectives of the school were accomplished should be assessed as accurately as possible. This information will be a valuable asset in beginning plans for VBS the coming year.

FOR REVIEW

1. What considerations are involved in leading a pupil to Christ?
2. Suggest ways pupils can be encouraged in Christian growth.
3. List three purposes of the closing program.
4. What three groups of people require follow-up?
5. State facts and information necessary for meaningful evaluation.

FOR DISCUSSION

1. How can a church help pupils who accept Christ as Savior? who decide to read the Bible and pray regularly? who commit themselves to full-time Christian service?
2. Discuss purposes of the following in a closing program: department presentations, testimonies of spiritual decisions, handcraft displays, pastor's comments.
3. How can contact begun with unchurched families whose children were in VBS be continued through the year?

FOR APPLICATION

1. Design an evaluation questionnaire for VBS staff to complete. If time allows, a second questionnaire might be prepared for pupils.
2. Collect materials to give VBS pupils that will encourage decisions for salvation, Bible reading, and service.

FOR ADDITIONAL ENRICHMENT

Soderholm, Marjorie. *Explaining Salvation to Children*. Minneapolis: Free Church Publications, 1979.